"*Predictive Leadership* is not theoretical mumbo jumbo. It helps you create an actionable step-by-step plan to move your business away from chaotic problem solving to proactive problem predicting. With that skill in place, achieving sustainable growth isn't luck or magic, it's simply execution. Dando's coached me on these concepts for years; this book puts his wisdom in an easy-to-digest format that every leader can benefit from."

—*Gabe Krajicek, CEO & Partner, BancVue,*
EY Entrepreneur of the Year, 2011

"Kirk has written a powerful, insightful book that will make you think, grow, and lead differently. Growth happens when you're challenged and uncomfortable, and Kirk certainly will challenge your strategies, beliefs, and willingness to make decisions. Any book that gets you willing to approach things differently is a winner in my book, and this is a winner."

—*Ben Decker, CEO, Decker Communications*

"Most business books and consultants typically tell you what you already know with few recommendations on how to remedy a problem. Not true with *Predictive Leadership!* Kirk's easygoing, non-threatening approach, plus his solid experience of successfully running large companies, makes *Predictive Leadership* a winner. It helped us take a number of issues we were experiencing caused by rapid growth and helped us focus on the three or four most critical issues."

—*Paul Bury, CEO, Bury*

"Kirk has demonstrated a unique ability to grow leaders at all levels in the organization. The insights in his book are essential for developing responsible leaders capable of both building high performing teams and driving sustainable, growth oriented businesses."

—*Ryan Robinson, former Human Resource VP, Hewlett*
Packard, and Chief People Officer, Bazaarvoice

"A good business book will provide insight, share actionable tools, or change behavior—*Predictive Leadership* does all three. It was amusing how Kirk described my struggles, knew exactly how I was feeling and the issues I was facing just like he had been there with me. Even better were the solutions and strategies that have helped me find a less turbulent, more fulfilling path to real success."

—*Alex Charfen, CEO, Charfen Institute*

"*Predictive Leadership* is a must-read for growing businesses who find themselves responding to circumstances instead of pouring their efforts into growth. *Predictive Leadership* will help put you out front where you belong. I intend to use these principles for my company."

—*Ken Davis, President of Dynamic Communicators Intl., bestselling author, radio host*

"Kirk has a knack for seeing company patterns that get them tripped up from their own successes. Knowing Kirk for years, he has the highest integrity and possesses a unique balance of emotional intelligence, strategic foresight, and detail-orientation."

—*Sam Decker, CEO, Mass Relevance*

"*Predictive Leadership* took us to a different place of discussion. It showed us that the opportunity and our current approach to that opportunity were NOT aligned."

—*Tim Hawks, Senior Executive Pastor, Hill Country Bible Church*

"Kirk believes that the best way to build leaders is to help them build the skills and experience they need to get to the answer on their own. Dando's advice helps give you the confidence to transition from problem solving to problem prediction. It has helped me be ready to predict a problem next time rather than diving into the weeds on a solution that only works today."

—*David Brussin, CEO, Monetate, EY Entrepreneur of the Year, 2012*

"Kirk's insights helped us focus our energies on 'working on the business.' Whether it's the team or strategies, everything is done in the context of how it drives business. If you truly do the work *Predictive Leadership* recommends, it will challenge you, your beliefs, your strategies, and your willingness to make the decisions necessary for the success of your business."

—*Paul Trylko, CEO, Amplify Federal Credit Union*

"It was a rude awakening for me to realize that while it takes the single-mindedness and zeal of an entrepreneur to develop a successful concept, it takes leadership to develop a successful company. And entrepreneurs aren't always accomplished leaders. If you're willing to tackle root cause and can get past the shock of discovering YOU ARE THE ROOT CAUSE, Kirk's teachings in *Predictive Leadership* can have a profound impact on your business."

—*John M Campbell III, Vice President, H-E-B Central Market*

"Dando's *Predictive Leadership* offers a no-nonsense approach to build strategies to reach our goals."

—*Bill Morrow, Executive Chairman & CEO, Quarri Technologies, EY Entrepreneur of the Year, 2010*

"With growth in our company, we realized we needed a change to reach the next level of success. What Kirk shares in *Predictive Leadership* enables us to take positive steps to implement the changes necessary for our future growth and success. I can, without hesitation, recommend Kirk Dando and *Predictive Leadership*."

—*Neel White, CEO, White Construction*

"Dando's experience and advice gives us valuable insights that have helped us avoid some of the pitfalls associated with both rapid growth and the ongoing evolution of our business."

—*Johannes Brinkmann, CFO, AM Technical Solutions*

"Change is very painful; *Predictive Leadership* helped us to prioritize so that the disruption has been minimal while the positive impacts have been remarkable."

—*Rocky Turner, CEO, LPR Construction*

"*Predictive Leadership* definitely speaks to, understands, and provides real world solutions to the key challenges you will face as you scale. Kirk really is 'the company whisperer.'"

—*Brett Hurt, Investor and Founder of Coremetrics and Bazaarvoice, EY Entrepreneur of the Year, 2009*

PREDICTIVE

LEADERSHIP

AVOIDING THE 12 CRITICAL MISTAKES THAT DERAIL GROWTH-HUNGRY COMPANIES

KIRK DANDO

palgrave
macmillan

First published in 2014 by PALGRAVE MACMILLAN® in the United States—
a division of St. Martin's Press LLC, 175 Fifth Avenue, New York, NY 10010.

Where this book is distributed in the UK, Europe and the rest of the world, this
is by Palgrave Macmillan, a division of Macmillan Publishers Limited, registered
in England, company number 785998, of Houndmills, Basingstoke, Hampshire
RG21 6XS.

Palgrave Macmillan is the global academic imprint of the above companies and
has companies and representatives throughout the world.

Palgrave® and Macmillan® are registered trademarks in the United States, the
United Kingdom, Europe and other countries.

ISBN: 978-1-137-27932-3

Library of Congress Cataloging-in-Publication DataDando, Kirk.

   Predictive leadership : avoiding the 12 critical mistakes that derail growth-
hungry companies / Kirk Dando.
     pages cm
   Summary: "Nothing masks issues and robs an organization of its full potential
like success That's right! Most successful, growth-hungry companies begin
to miss their projections or worse, not because demand is low or conditions
are difficult, but simply because they don't know how to predict, nurture, or
even maintain their own growth and success. At each stage of growth, natural
problems are glossed over in the scramble to expand, making the organization
vulnerable to chaos, no matter how strong or expert its leaders. Most leaders feel
isolated, pressured to build on earlier success and maintain total control—the
perfect recipe for the 12 most common and critical mistakes to show up and
slow or kill growth.Kirk Dando, leadership and growth expert, CEO of Dando
Advisors, calls these roadblocks the "12 Warning Signs of Success," and has
helped leaders across industries predict, prepare, and avoid them at every stage of
growth. Predictive Leadership is rich with real-world stories, prescriptive advice
on how to scale your business and limit the drama so you can unlock the growth
and success you desire.Maybe you had the right idea but hired the wrong person.
Maybe you're running into a leadership bottleneck, having trouble getting your
team aligned, unknowingly incentivizing failure, or losing sight of your core
values. Dando, known in leadership circles as the "Company Whisperer," has
encountered every one of these obstacles himself, as a C-level executive in a high-
growth billion-dollar business. He knows firsthand that these moments of truth
determine whether you can lead your company to become a strong, mature, and
financially sustainable organization, or drift toward an uncertain future."
—Provided by publisher.
   Summary: "Leadership and growth expert Kirk Dando points out the most
common mistakes successful businesses make while scaling up—and how to
avoid them"—Provided by publisher.
     ISBN 978-1-137-27932-3 (hardback)
     1. Leadership. 2. Small business--Growth. 3. Success in business. I. Title.
HD57.7.D3563   2014
   658.4'092—dc23

                                                                    2014011174

A catalogue record of the book is available from the British Library.

Design by Letra Libre Inc.

First edition: May 2014

10 9 8 7 6 5 4 3 2 1

Printed in the United States of America.

To my three loving daughters:
Lauryn Dando, McKenna Dando and Sloan Dando

CONTENTS

ACKNOWLEDGMENTS

WORDS CANNOT BEGIN TO DESCRIBE THE GRATITUDE I HAVE for the individuals in my life who saw the potential in me that I did not see in myself. A handful of coaches, teachers, employers, clients, friends, pastors, board members, family members and colleagues have selflessly invested in me for no other reason than to help and support me. These are the individuals whom I owe so much, but they helped me with no expectation of reciprocation or compensation . . . true leaders!

In regard to getting this book done, there are three people to whom I want to extend a special thank-you:

- Cindy Osburn
- Rusty Fisher
- Leigh Choate

A deep level of gratitude goes to these three for their support and encouragement!

INTRODUCTION

I'VE BEEN THERE—HERE'S HOW
THIS BOOK CAN HELP YOU

I'VE BEEN THERE.

What makes this book unique is that I am going to help you *predict, prepare and normalize* your leadership and growth journey. I have walked in your shoes. I have learned many of these lessons and discovered the best solutions the hard way. Whether you're leading a small start-up or an established international company, you'll see yourself in these pages.

I am going to share a little bit about my background because I believe it is important that you understand *how* I am hard wired, *what* drives me and *why* I am so passionate about what I share in this book.

I want you to know you have a *friend in the foxhole*, someone who has gone before you and is now coming back to help you grow and scale . . . without all the drama. I have practiced, researched, applied and exploited the patterns of what the world's most successful leaders do differently, the warning signs of their success and how to predict the risks and opportunities before they show up in the results, when it is too late.

I learned a long time ago how to read the tea leaves; to see past the glare and figure out what's really there; to cut through the chaff and get straight to the heart of the matter. I did this out of necessity, driven by fear and the survival instinct.

I was born in Englewood, Colorado, to a schoolteacher father and a stay-at-home mom, and my life was fairly predictable until I was in the fourth grade. That year, my parents divorced. All of a sudden, my life was in free fall, and I was trying to patch together a parachute on my way to the ground. The sudden pain, uncertainty and loss left me doubting everything and everyone, including myself.

Those words, "we are getting a divorce," broke me and up-ended me in ways that changed me to the core. I had no idea my parents were even unhappy. How could I not have seen this coming? What did I miss? Could I have helped avoid this crisis, this intense fear and pain I was feeling, if I had somehow seen it coming?

I did not know it at the time, but this profound pain and the irrational idea that I could have done something to help save my parents' marriage if I had recognized the warning signs set me on an unplanned journey that has ultimately served both me and thousands of other leaders extremely well.

Although my story is not your story, I think you will find that we are not all that different. As you read this book, I believe you will come to appreciate and understand the significance of this overly obvious and embarrassingly simple truth.

I have worked with and coached over 5,000 growth-hungry leaders. I have helped lead and grow a business to $1 billion in annual revenues. I have seen the rational and irrational thought processes behind literally millions of decisions, sat in and facilitated countless strategy sessions, been in extremely volatile board meetings and seen entire executive teams get fired. I have sat at the right hand of some of the world's most recognized leaders while they had major victories and when they had major breakdowns that exposed rawness and vulnerability that few others get to see. This has helped give me a true insider's view of how high-growth leaders succeed and what *really* goes on inside their organizations.

Keep reading—I will explain how my story, my journey and what I have learned can serve you well, too!

PART I

A LEADER'S JOURNEY

THIS BOOK IS ABOUT HELPING *YOU* GROW AS A LEADER AND helping you predict and prepare for success. I will help bust open the isolation so many leaders feel when growing their team and their organization by shedding light on the sweet little lies success tells you. You will have the logic and data to take the drama out of the journey of leading a great organization that truly changes the world. In this book I will teach you how to navigate the obstacle course that success and growth will inevitably present.

You will hear me say this numerous times in this book: *Your details may be different, but the dynamics that growth and success cause are always the same.*

Once you understand this important distinction, in business as well as in life, you will see beyond your details and see to the patterns that will enable you to become a predictive leader. You will lead way beyond telling and analyzing the "what happened and why" story; you and your team will be all about "what's coming." This is what the 12 Warning Signs of Success are all about!

At age 10, faced with the new reality of a broken family, I set out on a journey that would lead to more loss, growth, learning and success than I could have ever imagined. I developed two skills in particular that have served me well in this journey of studying leadership, growth and success. First, I began to pay attention to the dynamics and the patterns in all my relationships. I learned how to read people: their motivations, what made them tick, what made them successful or tripped them up. Second, I developed a "never say die," contrarian mentality that drove me to accomplish whatever I set out to do—and prove naysayers wrong. This is the rocket fuel that has driven me to research what is often considered to be mystical and theoretical—success and growth. I had to know, are there patterns found in historical and transactional data that can be exploited to help predict success and growth?

One of my earliest memories of trying out this latter skill was when my big brother, Kevin, bet me (who knew me too well) I could not outrun a BB from my Daisy pump-action BB gun. I remember thinking, "I cannot possibly say no, but maybe if I run in a zigzag pattern, he will miss and I can *claim* I outran the BB." Well, he didn't miss. Feeling the sting of the BB on my skin, I remember resolving to never let others define me and determine what I could or could not do. Even after the bruising went away it never occurred to me that trying to out run a BB from a BB gun was a bad idea, it just made me mad and more driven!

After high school I was told that I was not good enough to play Division 1 football, so I walked onto the football team at Colorado State University and earned a full-ride scholarship to play football for four years. While at CSU, the only class I did not get an "A" in during my freshman year was accounting, so I decided to make it my emphasis in my business major. From the beginning, whatever people—coaches, teachers, colleagues, relatives—told me I couldn't do was what I wanted to do to prove them wrong.

Since successful leadership requires a certain kind of personality, I'm guessing this habit of getting in way over my head is one that you share or can relate to.

After graduation, through sheer determination and relationship management, I got the opportunity to work for Arthur Andersen in the audit division. I am so grateful for this opportunity and what I learned. I worked with a variety of businesses, helping them grow and improve. It was pretty normal stuff, but what fascinated me most were all the leaders in all the companies I observed and learned from. I remember thinking, "There has got to be a pattern that determines what makes a leader successful—or a mess," and I resolved to figure it out! The same irrational resolve I have been explaining to you.

I began watching, reading and learning from some of the world's most recognized leaders, both good *and* bad. I would even study them when we went to dinner: how they treated the wait staff; how many people in the restaurant they knew; whether they could remember a colleague's first name and the names of family members—not just the spouse.

I was part of a pretty big team, and we provided written strategic, practical, organizational and personnel recommendations to our clients about what their companies needed to do in order to improve and grow. But I always wondered why we never just sat down and had the awkward and scary conversations—for example, telling the CEO that the CFO or VP of sales was a jerk, a poor leader who was actually hurting the company's ability to put a winning team on the field. I figured either the senior partners and managers were having those conversations and I simply wasn't part of them, or I was just young and had a lot to learn about what worked best in the advice-giving business.

Yet when we showed up at the same company a year later, the same people were still in the same positions, very few of our recommendations had been implemented and the company's situation was worse, not better. This frustrated me to no end, for I believe that if you are going to play, why not play to win? Firing a brilliant jerk was well within our mandate to recommend and the CEO's responsibility to handle. Why didn't it happen until there was a crisis? And believe me, the crisis always came eventually.

HOW TO BECOME A PREDICTIVE LEADER

Once again, I share these stories not just to give you the details of my life but also to help you recognize that the patterns and problems of success and growth are *all the same.*

So if you can see past your details (the stories and examples), you will see the patterns of how to become a predictive leader who wins rather than repeating the same critical mistakes of thousands who have gone before you.

While I was at Arthur Andersen, I was tapped to be chief financial officer for a growing company. I'd never been a CFO before, though I knew my way around a set of financials. Smart people know that the *F* in CFO is the easy part. It's the C part that takes real intelligence, experience and leadership.

And let me tell you, I did not have them.

At least, not then.

But I did have two things, thanks to my past: a deep need to help people so they did not have to hurt and feel insecure the way I did, and a relentless curiosity about where I could have the biggest impact. My "never say die" mentality served me well once again, as I swore not to rest until I figured the job out.

What I found was that the most significant way to help people is by being an effective *leader,* not only in business, but also in school, at church, at home, in sports and everywhere else.

Everywhere I looked I noticed the impact and influence leaders have. The frustrating part was that I was exposed mostly to ineffective leaders and the damage they could do to an individual, a team and ultimately the organization they were supposed to be serving.

One of the people I admire, John Maxwell, sums it up so well when he says, "*Everything* rises or falls on leadership."[1]

I remember my first few days as a CFO like they were yesterday. I remember the CEO coming into my office and telling me that if we did not turn things around, he was going to shut the firm down. He did not really mean it; he was just expressing his frustration. But of course I didn't realize that. I remember thinking, "Wow, I need to get a lot better at asking questions in the interview!" And then I had an even scarier, second thought: "If he is telling me about this, then he expects me to do something about it!" I came to find out the second thought was not necessarily true.

When I dug into the problems the business was facing, I saw a lot of issues. To me, many of them were overly obvious and embarrassingly simple; later I found out that obvious and simple do not mean easy.

We had several offices in various locations: many of them were run independently; some were successful, others weren't; all were run and accounted for slightly differently and the corporate office was viewed to some extent as useless overhead charged to these overburdened offices. I knew enough to recognize that this was neither good nor bad—just likely inefficient. What I wanted to know was, what were the most successful leaders doing that the others weren't?

In other words, what were the patterns that led to success?

But first we had to determine exactly who was "successful." That may sound odd, but I learned that there were no real metrics in place to measure success. One office had great sales but huge overhead. Another office struggled to perform basic tasks that were a breeze at corporate. Still another office leader was charging personal groceries to the office account and was offended when I asked why.

So I started asking questions. I brought together leaders from the disparate offices to see how they ran their businesses, how they defined success and what we could learn from one another.

You can probably guess what happened, and maybe you're even grinning at my naïveté. That's right: Nobody wanted to have to answer to the new kid on the block who had volunteered to take on the job of chief operating officer in addition to CFO.

People were defensive; their feathers were ruffled. In short, it was a mess. Those were some of the loneliest, most stressful days of my working life. Most of my decisions were judged in a vacuum and taken out of context. I had few friends at the office—most people were happy with the status quo and couldn't fathom what I was trying to accomplish even though the CEO and I had explained *why* things needed to change countless times. Because they doubted me, I doubted myself, but I cared too much—and my curiosity was too highly piqued—to stop.

So I read books, talked to business coaches, looked to board members and consultants for help. There were many long, lonely drives home late at night, followed by sleepless nights during which I told myself the sweet little lies that at the time I did not realize were neither necessary nor helpful. I wish someone had pointed out that the concerns I had were actually just by-products of our success, that they were normal; then I could have gotten my head back in the game a lot quicker.

But I did not quit. I kept asking questions.

Slowly but surely, we consolidated the best practices and found economies of scale for all the offices. We streamlined our operations, which helped our bottom line. We focused on fewer key products and services to maximize revenues. We made tough decisions about the management team, letting even long-term employees go. *It was gut wrenching, and it got worse before it got better.*

But we made it. The team's annual sales hit $1 billion for the first time ever, which set the company up for a successful sale, and it was all worth it.

I learned that the road to heaven most definitely goes through hell . . . and it's worth it! I also learned that it is your choice if it is a day trip or a daily trip. Ultimately, I learned a lot more about growth than about success from this process. Although the outcome was good, the journey had much more drama than was necessary.

Once the company was sold, I had time to think about what I really wanted to accomplish with my professional life. It all came back to those defining qualities: a desire to help others and intense curiosity about leadership, growth and success.

I realized that, around the world, every business leader— or community leader, church leader, family leader, any kind of leader—went through the same doubt, anxiety, fear, gut wrenching decisions and dread. And all those emotions were most likely the by-products of success rather than failure.

I've coached more than 5,000 business leaders over the past 17 years and built my own successful business, and I've seen it all: crazy decision making based on fantasies (or worse, ideas from your father-in-law!); hiring practices that make everyone your best friend . . . but sink your finances and crush your dreams. I've seen things stunk up in almost every possible way.

And I've helped turn those businesses around.

I've learned that change is inevitable, but growth is a choice.

So I know exactly how you feel when you want to cry or give up or just *fire everyone*. And I wrote this book so you have fewer long, lonely drives home.

THE 12 WARNING SIGNS OF SUCCESS

The truth is, there are 12 critical mistakes that almost every leader and their team make. I call them the 12 Warning Signs of Success. These mistakes can cause a lot of pain and slow business growth—at best. At worst, they cause businesses—and sometimes fortunes—to disappear.

But they're all avoidable because, believe it or not, they're predictable.

In this book, I'll show you exactly what the best leaders do differently to avoid these blind spots. You'll understand how a "signal of success" can actually be a sign of disaster to come. For example, a great quarter with higher-than-projected revenues may seem like a good reason to break out the champagne. But when you sober up, you realize you have no reliable way to predict sales or anything else for that matter; it just happened to work out in your favor . . . this time. Or you discover that when your fledgling company nabs a top C-level executive from that huge publicly traded company, you've actually hired a diva that hides behind the work of her many drones.

When you can read the signs—good and bad—it's a lot easier to steer clear of the wreckage.

I'm not here to tell you you're Superman or Wonder Woman and you can do it all. The fact is, you cannot *effectively* lead beyond where you have already been. When I was a CFO/COO, it wasn't just that I didn't know what to do in those positions. I didn't know *what* I didn't know. I could likely handle the spreadsheets, P&Ls, and office expenses but I could not see into my own blind spots and recognize the patterns of what I had never seen or experienced before.

Before we get started, however, let's talk about how best to make this book work for you.

ONE

MY PROMISE TO YOU

HOW TO MAKE THIS BOOK ACTIONABLE

SO NOW YOU KNOW I'M NOT PERFECT, I'M NOT A GENIUS, *YOU* are not alone and I'm certainly honest about my intentions. I'm about to make you a promise about this book, so read on.

I think you will find that the ideas in this book are very contrary—with one exception—to the typical attitudes in leadership and business today. The one exception is the group of leaders and businesses that I have had the privilege of being associated with and who have learned many of these successful ideas. Now, let's get started.

As we begin this critical journey, I make you one simple promise. We've all opened books with high hopes, only to be disappointed. We've learned that implementing advice is like wrestling with a ghost: It is really hard to do. Some of us may even have shelves full of unread books or abandoned audiotapes that we cannot figure out how to apply to our own "unique" situations.

The fact is, *information alone does not change anything.* If it did, we would all be rich, skinny and happily married.

Real behavioral change typically results from one of two things: We either have a crisis or we predict one! Now, I shared with you one of my crises: my parents' divorce, which forced me to change my thinking and my behavior. The better way to grow and change is to predict the crisis, visualize the fallout and, without creating drama, head it off before we have to clean up the mess. Guess which one 90% of leaders like to do . . . wait for the crisis!

So I challenge you now. The only way you will gain anything from this book is to do two things:

1. *Be honest.* Tell yourself the truth. Ask others in your life to tell you the truth as you go through this book and start to ask questions. You can fool everyone else, but do not fool yourself. *If you're not ready to face the truth*—then put this book down. Pick it up when you have your next crisis, when you have to face the truth and are ready to change your behaviors for good.

2. *Take action.* You can't simply read a diet book and expect to lose 20 pounds. Similarly, you can't read this book, file the information away and hope for the best. You will undoubtedly find at least one challenge in this book that your company is facing right now or that you can see coming. I'll give you step-by-step guidance, illustrated by examples (names changed to protect the innocent), on how to deal with it. But it's up to you to take action. I'm not expecting you to leap tall buildings in a single bound or climb Mount Everest wearing flip-flops and swim trunks. But if you're not ready to do *something,* put this book down until you are.

If you *are* ready to be honest and you *will* take action, I guarantee you will experience the following life-changing events:

1. You will see and understand the *obvious* and *simple* answers that will help you grow, mature and stabilize your business. In fact, you will wonder why you never saw them before.

2. You and your team will become *predictive leaders* rather than *problem solvers*. You won't believe the time, resources and worry you'll save by dealing with problems before they ever materialize. This fact alone is worth the time it takes to read this book.

3. You and your team will *use your time and talent* to craft new products and services for your market, rather than wasting them solving common problems that have already been solved by thousands of other businesses.

4. You will *redefine* what the journey to growth looks like for you, your team and your business, creating a wealth that is far more satisfying than money alone.

5. You and your team will *unlock* the opportunities you have been missing so you can get busy *changing the world*.

Sound crazy? Ambitious? Does it make you nervous? Great! Then we're in the sweet spot between skepticism and belief, between doubt and change!

Don't worry—I'll be here to help every step of the way.

HOW TO MAKE THIS BOOK ACTIONABLE

By definition, successful leaders don't take just any action; they take the *right* action. I know you're busy; I am too. So make the most of the time you're investing in this book. The *principles* of leadership are constant, but the application of those principles is what separates the true leaders from the posers. The strategies and principles I share in this book are the same ones I used with several CEOs of the Year and Ernst and Young Entrepreneurs of the Year. But only you can bring the desire and motivation to apply what I am teaching you.

Without your desire and motivation, nothing *can* or *will* change.

Decide not to be like all the others who read books in the hope of confirming their existing positions or perceptions. Read with an open mind.

You must be absolutely committed to building new strategic muscles and letting some old ones atrophy.

And when you're done, you'll understand how to *predict* and *prevent* future train wrecks in your business, allowing you to focus your precious energy on creating breakthrough products and services that fuel your growth.

Ready? Here are four simple steps to make this book actionable from the very beginning.

Step 1: Determine Where You, Your Team and Your Business Are in Your Business's Growth Cycle

Carefully note the characteristics and growth strategies that describe businesses at Levels 1, 2 and 3 (see Part II).

What you will learn in Part II: Once you understand where your business is in the growth cycle, you will have the context and talking points to predict and prepare your team for the issues that growth and success cause in all *successful* businesses. This subtle but significant leadership skill will increase your team's confidence in you, so when hard times hit (and they will), your team will trust you to lead them through or around the crisis.

For example, let's say you and I were getting ready to climb Mount Everest and you knew I had already climbed Mount Everest several times before. This should make you feel confident in my abilities, right? Now, how would you feel if we got halfway up the mountain and you realized I did not tell you that you were going to need extra oxygen or that you needed to bring special equipment for the severe weather? If I did nothing to predict the very predictable issues we would encounter when climbing Mount Everest, you would start to seriously lose confidence in me as each obstacle arose. Instead of focusing on getting to the top, you would probably start to worry about getting back down alive.

Now, imagine if I instead completely prepared you for every situation that could occur along the way. What if I told you that there might be times when we stop climbing, even though the weather is great, because I know the clouds way off on the horizon will unleash a storm on us at a point where we will not be able to set up camp? And what if I told you each morning about the nature of the next stretch and what it might require of us, all of which turned out to be true? You would start to trust me, but more important, you would stay focused on the task at hand, which is how you successfully reach the goal, getting to the top. Moreover, if a truly unpredictable crisis arose, you would most likely attack it with grit and determination because you would give me *the benefit of the doubt* and retain your faith in my ability to lead you the rest of the way.

It is no different leading a team in a business that wants to grow. If we can predict the most common problems that growth and success cause, then why do so many leaders and their businesses fail to describe and normalize the journey for their teams? Instead, most get caught off guard and then wonder why they start to feel isolated and alone. This leaves their most talented people wondering why their leaders seem so lost, and their confidence begins to waver. They are no longer playing to win, but rather trying not to lose; they turn their attention to managing their careers rather than the company. They most likely start caring more about getting out with their reputations intact than about keeping the company intact.

The business's growth cycle is going to give you the context and talking points you need to prepare and successfully lead your team up the mountain of growth and success.

Step 2: Review the 12 Warning Signs of Success

You will find the 12 Warning Signs of Success in Part III. These are the 12 most critical mistakes growth-hungry leaders make, and each is a direct result of an earlier success. Each warning sign of success follows the same template; use it to delve deeper into whether or not you have this warning sign of success and what to do about it.

What you will learn in Part III: By understanding and following the prescriptive advice I give for each warning sign of success, you and your team will learn to:

- Focus on the *vital few* growth strategies that will actually help you scale your business, and avoid getting paralyzed by the *trivial many*.
- Clearly identify the current realities of your leadership capabilities, your business and your future growth potential.
- Understand how to build, burn or reinforce the bridges necessary for you to move from where you are to where you want to be—without train wrecks.

Step 3: Have the Courage to Start a Conversation

Discuss with your leadership team and your board of directors (if you have one) what needs to happen for your business to grow.

Honor them with the same honesty and compassion that you gave yourself, recognizing their contributions in the past and knowing that change alone can be the biggest challenge for many of your people. Honesty is not only the best policy; it's the *only way* you will be able to lead your team and grow your business to the next level.

At the end of the day it is not what happens *between* you and your team but what happens *through* you and your team!

Step 4: Be Determined to Become a Predictive Leader Instead of a Problem Solver

The overarching purpose of this book is to help leaders predict, prepare and take the drama out of the journey of building a successful leadership team and business. This book will challenge you and subsequently arm you with the ability to *predict* and prepare for problems *before* they show up in the results.

MOVING FORWARD . . .

The real aha will come when you compare your journey with the characteristics or warning signs of success and the stories of others who have gone before you. This will allow you to learn from others, rather than struggling by yourself.

You'll see that you're not alone. I've learned that you get what you set yourself up for. Do you *really* know what you are setting yourself up for? By the end of this book, you will.

Let's go!

TWO

WHY LEADERS NEED WARNING SIGNS OF SUCCESS

THE DIRTY LITTLE SECRET ABOUT SUCCESS—IS YOUR SUCCESS ACTUALLY SIGNALING YOUR FAILURE?

ONE IMPORTANT THING FOR LEADERS TO REMEMBER: A LOT OF what looks like chaos actually isn't. As leaders, we like to blame our problems on the shifting state of the world, with comments like, "Things are changing so quickly, it's impossible to keep up," or, "Do I or my team have what it takes?" The truth is, we tend to *give in* to what we see as chaos. When we do that, we subconsciously *give up* on the possibility of predicting the problems before they show up in the results. We tell ourselves that there will inevitably be crises, large or small, that we'll just have to stop and deal with.

No one ever talks about the dirty little secret that *some results that look like success* (hiring more staff, increasing revenues, outgrowing facilities, beating goals, etc.) *often breed failure,* and that's what sets up the chaos. I'm here to tell you that the environment can be harnessed, and this book will show you how.

What most growth-hungry leaders want is to *get and stay* on top. What they do not realize is that the journey they think they are on will not get them where they want to go.

The sweet little lies we leaders tell ourselves eventually turn into big bad doubts that threaten our capacity to lead. The 12 Warning Signs of Success will help you see that you are not alone in your rationalizations—but they are often at the heart of your greatest train wrecks.

The sweet little lies are the stories all leaders tell themselves so they do not have to face issues head-on. The big bad doubts are the whopper lies leaders tell themselves that make them too paranoid for their own good.

This seemingly endless quest to get ahead of the learning curve and gain knowledge they know they do not have sends even the most confident and seasoned leaders on a scavenger hunt for information about what others have done to make their journey successful. They join leadership groups that meet regularly, talk to their friends in similar situations, and so on, only to find that compiling a lot of pithy platitudes, alliterative advice and non-actionable ideas is like wrestling with a ghost: It's hard and you cannot stop when you are tired; you have to wait for the ghost to get tired.

This quiet yet violent emotional stir amplifies the "it's lonely at the top" mentality. It also produces subtle but profound behaviors that cause leaders to *unknowingly* restrict their businesses' growth (playing it safe vs. playing to win).

In short, too much of the wrong information—oftentimes information leaders tell themselves—can paralyze even the best leaders. And you can never win if you don't move.

Look, I'm not here to bring you down. But the last thing you need right now is to hear another pack of lies—"the sweet little lies"—about success. You and I both know it's going to take more than "3 Secrets," "4 Strategies," "5 Keys," "6 Rules," "or "7 Magic Beans" for you to succeed. And a few indicators of "success" may not be true indicators at all. What you need is a book that sheds light on *the lies success will tell you.*

The biggest dirty little secret is that growth and success often court failure. For every Steve Jobs, Richard Branson, Bill Gates, Oprah Winfrey, and Mark Cuban, there are hundreds of thousands of people who failed miserably and will never be the same. It doesn't mean they were not capable, but I suspect they simply weren't *ready* for the harsh reality of business success: How to find it, how to grow it and—ultimately—how to keep it.

That's right; one of the harshest realities about success is that not everyone who finds it gets to keep it. Too often, once your company has had "success," its continued success seems like a foregone conclusion: once a success, always a success. But you quickly learn that it's not at all true. So rather than fighting to keep their success or struggling to grow it, most people struggle just to *maintain* it.

Instead of trying to stop problems before they happen, many successful people simply wait for problems to crop up and struggle to solve them, while falling behind on other, forward-looking initiatives.

Do either of the following two scenarios sound familiar? Rather than realizing that meetings are going longer and longer and solving less and less, you simply endure them until everyone is physically there but otherwise on a mental field trip: Little gets done. Instead of holding that lackluster team member or brilliant jerk accountable, you simply endure him or her until the situation finally blows up in your face.

I'm here to tell you that ignoring these problems doesn't just make the problems worse; it can cause really smart people on the team to get frustrated, feel unappreciated or sink to the level of mediocrity that surrounds them. Your best and brightest may end up napping on your dime or leaving to work for the competition . . . or worse, become the competition!

GRAVY TRAIN OR TRAIN WRECK?

In this book I'll refer to what I call a "train wreck," a concept adapted from one of my mentors, John Maxwell. Here's how I think of it: The cars sitting on the tracks have great value because they're loaded with different but valuable cargo (like team members: They're all different but collectively valuable); they have a destination (the vision, measurable goals and expected time frames for arrival at the goals); and they have a route to follow (the mission and strategic plan). But they do not have a way of getting anywhere on their own. They have to hook up to the engine (the leader).

Have you ever watched how a bunch of railcars (the team) form a working train? It all begins with the engine (leader). The engine switches itself to the same track as the car (team member) it's going to pick up; then it backs up to the car, makes contact and connects. Then it repeats the process until it has all the cars and starts heading toward its destination, sometimes picking up more cars along the way.

Likewise, all leaders are conductors, steering their corporate "trains" onward, upward and ever forward with knowledge, experience, confidence and enthusiasm—and, above all else, passion and a sure and steady hand.

So, given that you're the conductor guiding your company around the next series of blind corners and long, stagnant stretches, exactly *what kind of train* are you running here?

Are you on . . .

- A runaway train to success;
- A train that once easily moved down the track with velocity but now struggles because it can't see the turns ahead; or
- A blissful cartoon train boogying along, completely unaware of the sharp, precipitous bend in the track that could leave you in an irretrievable wreck?

As the conductor in charge of your company's success or failure, you need to know each bend in the track (the map of your company's journey), the altitude of every mile (what others before you have already discovered), the weather forecast and how it could impact you (competitive threats or market changes), how many passengers your "train" can hold (how big your company should get) and when to pick up steam (go fast) and when to keep things slow and steady.

Oh, and anything else that could go awry.

So have you ever conducted a train this size before?

OKAY, TAKE A MINUTE TO CATCH YOUR BREATH. You'll need it, because in this section I'm going to warn you about the 12 most critical and deadly business train wrecks that could derail your journey to success. I call them "warning signs of success" because these are the most common challenges that can suddenly slow previously successful organizations way down, or launch them on a gut-wrenching roller coaster of bravado and uncertainty.

It may be your first day on the job at your first company, or your thousand and first day on the job and your tenth company, but the warning signs—and potential train wrecks—are all the same.

Your job as "conductor" is to steer your company in the right direction.

No company is immune to failure, just as no train is wreck-proof. Some pitfalls can be avoided because of your company's lack of size. Others you encounter *because* of your company's size—as your company grows, unfamiliar circumstances breed new challenges. Regardless of how experienced you are as a leader or how big or small your company is, every one of these warning signs is indicative of something we normally celebrate: *success!*

IS YOUR SUCCESS ACTUALLY SIGNALING YOUR FAILURE?

Why do I call these the 12 *Warning* Signs of Success? The answer is simple: If you don't heed them, the very things that cause your success can also cause your demise.

They can appear at any and all stages of leadership development and business growth. Over the next three sections, I've organized them by defining elements, such as the processes a team uses to achieve its goals, the people on the team and the team's metrics and accountability (or lack thereof).

So here's a preview. I've grouped the signs under the three key challenges of any growth-hungry company, namely, leadership, culture and performance:

Leadership: Is My Leadership "Train" the Problem?

The First Warning Sign of Success: Right Idea, Wrong Person

You started out with the right ideas, right people and right direction, but somewhere along the way, you ended up with the wrong people in key positions. Your employees changed (or maybe you needed them to change and they didn't or wouldn't), you changed or your goals changed. Whichever it is, some of the key people you hired are now liabilities. It's tough—and personal!—to think about making changes, but you must. So you go to great lengths to identify what you need, hire a recruiter, and land that soon-to-be superstar—only to find out you once again have hired or promoted the wrong person. How do you keep this from happening, or at least reduce the chances of it? How do you change key players without losing momentum? And how do you sleep at night while all this is costing you time and money? I will show you the answers to these questions and the many other challenges faced in this first warning sign of success.

The Second Warning Sign of Success:
Bad Management of Great Opportunities

Rarely is it actual lack of opportunity that causes a business to struggle or fail; more often, it is bad management or poor prioritization of existing opportunities. As a company grows, long-term employees are "rewarded" with managerial leadership roles—whether or not they have the necessary skills or experience. Teams simply grow up around technical superstars. Some will thrive in management positions, but others will fall back to their comfort zone—working *in* the business instead of *on* the business. Then you have a real problem: Your employees are not able to take advantage of all the opportunities in front of them because they are so frustratingly mismanaged. How do you demote or replace the same people who were at your side from the very beginning and helped you be successful to this point? How do you reward loyalty so everyone (the business, you, the team, key stakeholders and the struggling team member) benefits? It's personal, emotional and debilitating. But if left unaddressed, this problem *guarantees* you'll never attain your highest potential; it's impossible without the right people in place.

The Third Warning Sign of Success: Open Door, Closed Mind

Your leadership team—including you!—says they're on board for change and growth, but their actions tell a different story. They dismiss ideas quickly or impede new processes. What were once a can-do attitude and a "playing to win" mentality have morphed into a "play it safe" mind-set. The leaders are not really listening to the rest of the team; they insist on doing it "their way," and the result is frustration. Negativity and insecurity seep in because the leader won't change course, even though failure is imminent (and avoidable!).

The Fourth Warning Sign of Success: Leadership Bottleneck

As CEO, you're expected to know it all. Every member of the leadership team reports to you, and all big decisions come through you. It's exhausting, but you're in charge, and it helps to have one single point of contact, "one throat to choke," right? Absolutely wrong. In fact, this kind of top-down organizational structure screams that you do not trust your managerial leaders, you're afraid of losing control, and you're throttling your business's growth. One likely consequence of this approach is the loss of some really smart managerial leaders. It can also destroy focus, as the CEO spends his time managing lots of people, rather than focusing on his strong suit (CEOs are usually technical geniuses, product gurus or incredible market builders, not great managers). This organizational structure is weak, unscalable and unsustainable. And it can't be fixed by simply adding one person "between" the CEO and the team. This one is tough but, like the others, completely avoidable . . . because it is predictable.

The Fifth Warning Sign of Success: Hope Is Not a Strategy

You and your team have set clear, measurable goals. It feels great—you know exactly what success looks like, and the future is bright. But there's a huge difference between a *goal* and a *strategy;* one is an endpoint, the other a complex process for actually getting there. Real strategy involves not just figuring out the 5% you will do, but identifying and saying no to the 95% you will not do. Many business leaders solve only short-term problems and call it "strategy." But real strategy takes time, brains and the long view—all of which can be difficult to conjure in the midst of a crisis. You can't hope your way to an audacious goal. Unlock your organization's full potential by preparing and executing effectively.

Culture: Where Is Your Culture "Train" Taking You?

The Sixth Warning Sign of Success: Core Values Meltdown

You started your company with nonnegotiable core values, performance expectations and culture, but they have slowly broken down over time. Compromises are made for special circumstances, brilliant jerks are tolerated—and your *actions* reveal your *actual* values. Your best employees lose faith, creating an "us versus them" environment. What changed, and why? How can you guarantee that your founding values and performance expectations remain front and center, no matter how your business veers or jostles? And how do you walk back from the compromises you have made?

The Seventh Warning Sign of Success: Drinking the Chaos Kool-Aid

Your business keeps you constantly energized. You see potential in new products, new markets—there's opportunity everywhere! You and your team go, go, go, and it's thrilling—for a while. But suddenly you're unable to say no or draw hard lines on where to spend your limited resources. The result is chaos: Your team is burned-out (and turning on you), you're stressed-out and, for all your effort, you feel like you're going nowhere. Your to-do list is endless—and also pointless. It is time to become ruthless about categorizing, prioritizing and getting laser focused on performance and measuring results.

The Eighth Warning Sign of Success: Communication Vacuum (aka It Sucks)

Despite countless emails, newsletters and meetings, employees consistently identify poor communication as a core problem. As your company grows, senior managers have less day-to-day interaction with operations and employees, so they're less aware of problems and priorities than they should be. Executives feel out of control, and employees perceive a lack of direction from the top. In fact, what we call poor communication is usually a mask for other, much deeper issues. What's *really* hiding behind "poor communication" in your organization?

The Ninth Warning Sign of Success: Incentivizing Failure

If leadership compensation isn't tied to the right metrics, you are rewarding mediocrity—or even failure—right now. Incentives that don't drive the right behavior or produce the desired outcomes erode employee confidence—and keep you off course for too long. Think about it: You have a few key employees who are superstars—they always solve problems that arise, and they do it well. But if your employees are spending their time problem solving, that means you're paying them *precisely not* to move the business forward, but rather to clean up messes that probably could have been avoided. Remember, you get more of what you reward. And those messes are keeping them from doing what you really need to do: drive growth.

Performance: What Is Our Performance "Train" Really Telling Us About Future Growth?

The Tenth Warning Sign of Success: The False Security of Revenues

Things look good; revenues are growing, so you relax a bit. But you have poor or spotty controls on spending, so you approve extra expenditures without much thought or analysis. And guess what? Your expenses start to grow faster than your revenues. You rein in spending—or worse, cut jobs—and you feel like you're in free fall. You don't have all the financial, performance or market data you need to predict problems—or you don't know how to analyze the data you do have. This has crushed far too many businesses—you likely know of several of them yourself.

The Eleventh Warning Sign of Success: Random Acts of Accountability

A lack of transparent, consistent accountability means that your top performers don't know exactly what to do, and less-than-great employees use the lack of an accountability culture to their advantage. You *should* be growing like crazy, but if you ask employees how they contribute to the end goals, you get a variety of answers—none of them quite right. It makes it even more maddening to make payroll each week. What are these people actually *doing?* Why don't they *get* it? Are you really paying all these people to *not* achieve the goals they committed to?

The Twelfth Warning Sign of Success: Sowing the Seeds of Decay

When you started out, you felt like you were ahead of the game because you created systems and processes that helped you get where you are today. But now your company has outgrown those systems and processes—everything from accounting to people to technology. And you may not even know it, because you're busy focusing on growing revenues or juggling rapid growth. It's counterintuitive, but systems that once enhanced your business are actually speeding its demise. This weakness will sneak up on you, killing your business from behind. Learn the signs of system and process decay *before* they start to impede your progress.

LEADERSHIP WHIPLASH!

As you can see—and your neck is probably sore from nodding so hard at many of these points—these 12 Warning Signs of Success reflect the most common, troubling and pervasive challenges leaders face. And they're all the direct results of personal or business success.

So now you know you are not alone. Not all signs of success have to do with landing that big new account or having huge, profitable years. Some signs of success are not fun, but they are just as much a sign of success as having 150% year-over-year growth. The real breakthrough happens when you can predict these Warning Signs of Success, prepare for them, minimize their impact, and sometimes avoid them altogether before they show up in the results. Keep reading, I am going to show you how.

Why only 12? It's because these 12 are the *root-cause* problems that can give birth to millions of "baby problems" that consume the time, attention and energy of well-intentioned leaders.

They're like the 12-point inspection every garage offers to ensure that your car is road ready. Ignore them at your peril, because just one rusty cable connection, worn spark plug or faulty gauge is enough to turn your next trip to the corner market into a four-figure trip to the nearest garage.

To grow consistently, you can't keep operating the same way you always have. Instead, you must double, triple, even quadruple the size and speed of everything in your firm. Yet many leaders allow the growth to happen without adjusting the environment accordingly. Unknowingly, they become the sand in the gears, even as others may loudly praise them for their "problem-solving" skills.

Ironically, if you focus on problem predicting rather than waiting for crises to hit, the size, speed and velocity of your business growth will take care of itself.

Let's take hiring, for example. As a small company, you could hire folks you knew or trusted from a fairly immediate pool of referrals. They worked hard, and well, because they were there at the start and believed in the company—and you.

But as you grow, you can't just keep looking for people you know or trust, or who believe in the cause, and then hope they will "get it" on the job. You need to look specifically for team members who have pure motives, are reliable, have sound judgment and are committed to consistent performance.

ARE YOU SOWING THE SEEDS OF DECAY? Trying to run a company with processes and systems that can't keep up is like building a bridge that can't handle the weight of the cars that will be crossing it. Subtly, over time, the processes and systems that were once the very reason for your growth have become the exact reason your business is struggling or running in place.

Many, many more people taste success, then fail, than *never taste success*. But the silver lining in this particular horror story is the secret for success that this book shares: By focusing on simplicity, fighting against complexity and becoming a *predictive leader* rather than a *problem solver*, not only can you master success; you can maintain it, harness it and grow it, too.

PART II

THE BUSINESS GROWTH CYCLE

GROWTH HAPPENS—WHERE IS YOUR BUSINESS IN ITS GROWTH CYCLE AND WHY DOES IT MATTER?

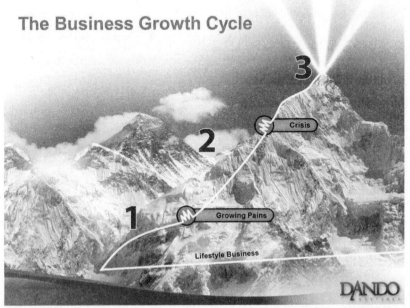

The Business Growth Cycle

3

Crisis

2

1

Growing Pains

Lifestyle Business

DANDO

Figure 1. The Business Growth Cycle is a model that helps leaders see where their business is performing now and precisely how to move to the next level.

LIKE ALL LIVING THINGS, YOUR BUSINESS HAS A *PREDICTABLE* growth cycle. Although how your team and your business experience growth is unique to your situation and industry, the issues that growth creates are common to everyone.

Likewise, the various components of your business may be at different stages of growth. This may require you to manage many of the challenges you'll learn about in this section—*at the same time*. Each stage begins with steady growth and stability and ends with a crisis that was predictable but ignored. Get ahead of that crisis and prepare your team so when the turmoil of change hits, they can respond appropriately.

Remember, you are the "conductor" of this train; if it wrecks or underperforms, it is because of you! This is very important to understand because when you acknowledge and absorb the truth of this statement, when you own this responsibility, you will take your first step in becoming a *predictive leader*.

There has *never* been a business whose growth was smooth, inevitable or linear; consider how much turnover there has been in the Fortune 500 companies over the years. Even if you're starting out today with nothing but a card table and a cell phone, you'll change and grow, and there will be rocky times. How do I know this? Because *all* successful businesses eventually grow themselves into problems! It is counterintuitive and frustrating but nonetheless a timeless truth, one that presents a unique opportunity if you will embrace it and use it to fuel your growth!

If you can *predict* how your business will grow, you can predict the problems before they show up in the results. This has a profound impact on helping lead your team and your company into and through the issues that all business growth creates.

Instead of having people turn on one another during times of "predictable" organizational turmoil, you will be able to foresee the growth tremors. Arming yourself with this knowledge will give your team and your board confidence in your leadership and will enable you to work as a team to navigate the business smoothly through the transitions.

Instead of allowing anxiety and raw emotions to fuel your business through tough times, you will now be able to tap into the passion, skill and unshakeable commitment of your team to *predict and prepare* for the 12 Warning Signs of Success before a crisis gets out of hand!

WHERE IS YOUR BUSINESS IN ITS GROWTH CYCLE?

While most of us intuitively recognize the various stages of business growth, I realized that if I was going to help my clients succeed in an actionable and measurable way, I had to do more than just know what business growth is; I had to define it.

My study began in earnest when I ran across an article by Larry E. Greiner called "Evolution and Revolution as Organizations Grow," which first appeared in the *Harvard Business Review*.[1] Robert (Bob) Beale of Beale International, who has been a thoughtful and wise mentor to me and many other entrepreneurs, further expounded on what he called his "four phases of business growth."[2]

Now, years after I began my study of business growth, I tried to build on their ideas and relate how successful businesses grow by using the analogy of climbing Mount Everest.

Most people have what it takes to get to base camp (start-up phase).

But *scaling* Mount Everest to the summit (like achieving rapid growth to become the market leader) takes incredible focus, knowledge, the help and experience of others who have done it before, commitment, training and *luck*. These are the tools you must have to attain sweet victory at the top, something that many dream of but precious few taste.

Frankly, it's the problem-predicting versus problem-solving part that makes my three stages of the business growth cycle both unique and complementary to these earlier versions.

The Business Growth Cycle is an approximate timeline of how an organization matures and the opportunities and problems that crop up at every stage. Avoiding these predictable pitfalls will help you become a market leader—presumably the objective of all growth-hungry leaders.

Too often, however, growth becomes not only an end in itself, but a company's modus operandi. The pursuit of growth overshadows customer service, research and development, branding, scalability, sometimes even survival.

It's a little like your first time on a social media site: All you care about is making connections, finding "friends," grabbing numbers and filling your wall with the profile pictures of random strangers.

Only later, when you truly come to value the one-on-one relationships that are the heart and soul of social media (or at least that should be), you realize you've grown larger than your capacity to share, contribute and collaborate. The same dynamic—a focus on quantity over quality—dooms many potential business relationships from the start.

This is where problem predicting becomes the foundation for growth. Armed with a sensitivity to and general understanding of the Business Growth Cycle, you can *predict problems* and prepare coping strategies so that no crisis gets big enough to drive you off track.

Each level begins with a period of steady growth and stability and ends with a period of substantial organizational turmoil and change.

Here's a bird's-eye view of what happens at each stage of the Business Growth Cycle. Because businesses are run by humans, it is not surprising that it strongly resembles the cycle of growth and learning most of us follow as people!

Step 1: Rebellion

In the beginning, things are going very well. We are experiencing steady growth and stability, so we tend to drop our guard. We're young, strong, invincible, immortal. Who needs sleep? We are at war! (With what or whom? Who knows?)

We think we have cracked the code on how to grow a business, and although we know, deep down, that our good luck cannot go on forever, we tell ourselves there is no stopping us!

I had a business leader call me who was in this first stage of rebellion. He ran a start-up printing company that got a huge contract from a major manufacturer. They were making approximately $200,000 in profit per month . . . and that was *after* the owners paid themselves a ridiculous salary. It was a huge coup and literally kept them going for years. They were on top of the world and couldn't see how this gravy train would ever end.

They focused most of their energy on this one client, neglecting to build processes and systems that could handle the weight and complexity of future growth and success. You can guess what happened: The purchaser at that huge client retired and was replaced by someone else. And that someone had a brother-in-law in the printing business.

Overnight, their huge customer was gone and the business was bereft. To an outsider the possibility that this would happen seems obvious, even inevitable. That's why it's critical to take a step back, listen to naysayers and honestly evaluate your situation. Otherwise, you put your business, all your employees and your customers at risk.

Step 2: Retribution

Next comes the fall, and it's a hard one. It's like having a great party in college, thinking the fun will never end. Then you wake up and realize you've wrecked your house, you can't find your wallet and your best friend isn't speaking to you. You overslept and missed your final. Your tuition money is missing. And guess what? Every single one of these problems could have been avoided. Poor choices result in chaos. Typically the decisions we make today do not play themselves out until later—sometimes years later. In the retribution phase, we start to sober up.

This is where blame and doubt seep in—and can crush your confidence while they crush your business. At such a low point, it's all too natural for leaders to tell themselves a few of those sweet little lies—"market conditions changed" (and we didn't predict them), "we had a crummy CFO" (who *hired* that CFO?), that huge customer took their business elsewhere (you didn't realize you only had one huge customer?). Some companies never finish making excuses, so they never make it out of this stage.

Step 3: Repentance

But not all leaders give up! Extreme hardship often triggers company-wide repentance, as you begin to refocus on what is *really* important. You're on your knees, down but not out. You clean up the house, have long, hat-in-hand conversations with your friends and professors and get a safe for the cash.

You put your ego in check. Teams and departments that may have squabbled before band together to get lean, cut budgets and do more with less. It's easier to see, in hindsight, where you went wrong.

You get rid of the lousy CFO, put a plan together to get new customers and vow to look more honestly at market changes, most of which are not as mysterious as you were pretending.

You admit you are part of the problem, and this truth sets you free. You're ready to move forward, a little bloody from the fight, but bright-eyed.

Step 4: Restoration

This is when we fully realize that, no, the company is not invincible, and the only way to survive is to realize that we're far from alone. Our business has the exact same problems as hundreds of other businesses that started in the rebellion phase and waited for a crisis to hit before they changed.

Guess what? We could stand to learn a little more from those who walked before us. We've matured, we've been humbled a bit and we're ready to get out of crisis/reaction mode and into the grown-up world of problem predicting.

The proof that we finally understand is that our projected growth starts to slow down—perhaps a lag in sales or hiring—and the pause allows us to catch our breath for another burst of growth.

We're tested and ready to move to the next level, a little wiser this time. This time, we're focusing on what's truly important.

THE CYCLE OF GROWTH AND LEARNING has run its full course (*rebellion, retribution, repentance* and *restoration*). If you and your team can embrace this fundamental truth—that failure is a natural part of growth and success—you will save yourself hours of hand wringing, closed-door bitch sessions, unnecessary self-doubt and embarrassing denial.

No company in history has had linear growth. Growth is not consistently smooth or inevitable. Your team should know that, without a doubt, you'll experience tumult, disappointment and potentially failure in the turbulence of growth—there's no avoiding them. If your team doesn't understand this, you need to explain it to them.

Chances are, you've lived through such turmoil before, regardless of which stage you're in at the moment. And if you haven't yet, you will very soon! Experience shows that only approximately *15%* of companies that grow from *Start-up* (Level 1) to *Hyper-Growth* (Level 2) succeed in making the transition to *Market Leader* (Level 3). The remaining 85 percent slide back and shrink, fighting the same battles day after day, until finally the business does not explode, the people do—often at one another. Or they burn too much cash and go out of business when they hit the crisis period between Level 2 and Level 3.

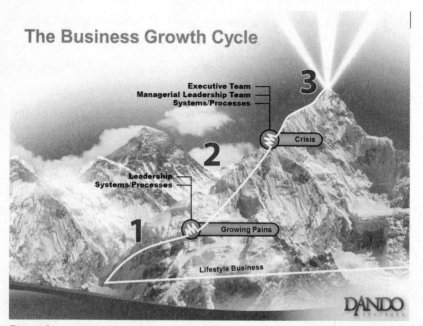

Figure 2

ONLY ACTIONS (NOT WORDS) GET RESULTS

Although very valuable, we must rely less on reporting *what has happened,* analyzing *why it happened,* monitoring *what is happening* and use the patterns found in this historical and transactional data to predict *what is going to happen.* Above all, we must act—not heedlessly or rashly, but based on key information gathered from trustworthy sources.

Moreover, we must be diligent in recognizing not just the attributes of each phase of growth, but also the transition that must naturally occur between phases.

That is why this section of the book is critical to your success and why the discussion of each phase of the Business Growth Cycle can help you reach the next.

Are You Climbing Mount Everest Out of Order?

The information in this section is designed to help you specifically identify where you are in the Business Growth Cycle. It may be a breath of fresh air to realize you're farther along than you thought—or a bucket of cold water to help you realize that you're in deep trouble. Either way, you need to know so that you can effectively deal with the problems that threaten to keep you from reaching that next level.

Many people are about as prepared to run a market-leading company as they are to summit Mount Everest. They show up at "base camp" (i.e., their first start-up company) in the climbing equivalent of flip-flops and a tank top, ready to rock and roll.

We all know that any fool with an idea and a tax ID number can start a business, but does that qualify them to run a market-leading company? Not any more than it qualifies a surfer to climb Mount Everest.

The fact is, it takes a certain amount of discipline, fore-thought, planning, perseverance and, above all, passion to climb the world's highest mountain. Becoming a market leader in your industry is really no different and *no less challenging.* You cannot reach the summit without these distinct skills.

What's more, what got you to base camp absolutely will not get you to the summit.

In fact, the higher you go up Mount Everest, the sharper your skills, focus and passion must be. Each step toward the summit increases your chances of death and decreases your chances of making it. It's not always the best climber who reaches the sum-mit. Instead, it's the most focused, prepared and passionate.

Becoming a market leader is no different. The skills that got you through your first year as a start-up are only an appetizer for the daily feast of injustices, inequities, market insecurities and fluctuation that faces you as you reach success on that level. It takes much more to sustain you at a higher altitude. (And it doesn't hurt if you can learn to predict changing weather patterns to help you decide when to climb and when to sit tight!)

The 3 Phases of Your Business Growth Cycle

The vertical axis in figure 3 illustrates where you'll see the evidence of growth in your company. What does that growth look like? Some of the indicators along our vertical/growth axis include:

- Increased revenue
- More demand for products and services
- More market presence
- More employees
- Larger office space and more offices

Figure 3. How a Business Scales

Along the horizontal axis in figure 3 you will see the issue of complexity, Time is the constant, always in the background.

I cannot tell you how often people tell me how worried they are about their competition. The reality is, you're your own biggest competition. Everyone has 24 hours in a day and seven days in a week, so it really is an even playing field. The winners figure out how to make the most of their money *and* their time.

Remember, all companies and their component parts (acquired or otherwise) are at different stages of development. Let's look at the three levels of possible growth.

THREE

LEVEL 1

START-UP

IT'S IMPORTANT TO RECOGNIZE THAT A START-UP COMPANY IS quite different from a company experiencing hyper-growth (although, if you're lucky, it often seems like both happen concurrently) and far removed from a Level 3, or market-dominating, company.

Beginnings are important, mainly because the personnel, habits and processes you put in place when you first start a company are the ones that will most likely make or break you. Remember: We get what we set ourselves up for.

This stage is probably the most fun, but it's also the most unpredictable. Perhaps you have always dreamed of being an entrepreneur, starting your own business; maybe you just finally got fed up with the nonsense of your job and decided to start your own business; or perhaps you just woke up and had an entrepreneurial seizure. No matter how you got here, it's exciting, if also a little terrifying.

You'll hear a lot about mission and vision at this stage, but they're mostly distractions. What is critical is your attitude toward and knowledge about business growth in general. Many businesses fail not because they can't handle growth, but because they're too insecure or unprepared for growth in the first place. During the start-up phase, it is obviously important to believe in your company—and yourself—but it's more important to implement the right disciplines and business basics, in the right sequence, from the very beginning.

Obviously, the main focus of a Level 1 business is to develop a product or service and sell it. At this moment, you are not focused on creating complex business systems and processes, onboarding a lot of new team members or building leadership development programs.

But someday, you will grow beyond the start-up phase and become a Level 2 business. And you must be at least aware of what that will entail. In figure 4, you can see what you need to think about now in order to keep growing. Please refer back to this chart as you read about level 2 and level 3. Think about how it applies to you and how you are leading and influencing your business.

Why waste brainpower designing and creating "stuff" to handle the weight of your growth, when that designing and creating has already been done and proven successful by thousands of other businesses during this phase? Instead, focus your brainpower on innovative ways to design new products and services that add true and lasting value for your customers!

If there is a good market for your products or services, you should grow yourself into the first inflection point. I call this inflection point "growing pains."

For a number of different reasons, conscious and subconscious, some leaders make the decision to remain a small business,

STRATEGIES FOR GROWTH-HUNGRY COMPANIES
Survival, Growth and Profitability Strategies

Priority	LEVEL 1	LEVEL 2	LEVEL 3
	1. *Survival* 2. *Growth* 3. *Profitability*	1. *Growth* 2. *Survival* 3. *Profitability*	1. *Profitability* 2. *Growth* 3. *Survival*

Survival	• Emphasize cash flow
	• Create viable products and/or services
	• Develop strong basic accounting:
	  - Monthly financial statements
	  - Cash flow projections
	  - Operating budget
	• Short term business plan
	• Identify and procure necessary funding
		• Emphasize cash flow
		• Secure additional funding
		• Develop incentive structure to motivate and reward superior performance
		• Create a strong management team
		• Expand and improve accounting systems to include operational performance measuring
		• Externalize
		  - Knowledge of economy
		  - Knowledge of own and related industries
		  - Knowledge about competition
		• Intermediate strategic plan for scaling business
			• Emphasize cash flow
			• Emphasize building an asset base
			• Emphasize executive leadership and management development
			• Create strong accounting, financial control, and financial performance reporting systems
			• Create strong work process systems
			• Create strong employee support and development systems
			• Expand externalization
			• Short and longer term business/ strategic plan
			• Emphasize timely, accurate assessment of competition

Growth	• Develop customer and revenue base which will survive indefinitely and can be built upon	• Expand market base and product line by plan, not by whim • Capitalize on product and market	• Expand into other market segments by plan • Emphasize new product development

STRATEGIES FOR GROWTH-HUNGRY COMPANIES (CONTINUED)
Survival, Growth and Profitability Strategies

	LEVEL 1	LEVEL 2	LEVEL 3
Priority	1. *Survival* 2. *Growth* 3. *Profitability*	1. *Growth* 2. *Survival* 3. *Profitability*	1. *Profitability* 2. *Growth* 3. *Survival*
Growth	• Define and cultivate the most viable markets within limits of financial resources, size, management ability, distribution capacity, etc. • Do not diversify into other businesses	knowledge and technical skills acquired in Level 1 • Do not diversify into other businesses • <u>Emphasize</u> acquiring and developing <u>the right</u> key personnel	and old product discontinuation • If diversification is a must, expand only into very closely related businesses which can capitalize on parent company's management, marketing and technical strengths
Profitability	• Owners must be committed to building a company rather than high personal income and free time • Make cash flow and growth more important than high profitability	• Increase profit rate, but plan to invest in longer term product and market development • Achieve adequate return on assets • Make building a viable organization more important than high profitability	• Achieve consistently strong profitability and return on assets • Strive to make company financially balanced to retain and attract outstanding middle and executive management and technicians • Make investment in people and systems a priority

Figure 4. Success Strategies for Growth-Hungry Leaders: Priorities at Each Level of Growth

what some call a "lifestyle" business. This is fine, *if* your true goal is to run a small, intimate company.

But if you secretly want to strive for more and decide to stay small because you refuse to face these Level 1 challenges, that's a problem.

How does a start-up start? It often grows out of frustration with the status quo. Entrepreneurs are frequently former employees of a Level 2 or Level 3 business in danger of failing or in a growth plateau. Do you have any of these employees in your Level 2 or Level 3 business, that are quietly making plans to escape for whatever reason? Would-be entrepreneurs see a different, better way of doing things but are frequently rebuffed by higher-ups.

Eventually they think, "If my ideas can't be appreciated here, I'll take them with me and start a company of my own." They gather around them a group of highly motivated, similar people and do exactly what they say they are going to do: start a company.

Starting a company is never easy, but I can tell you from experience that it sure is fun. Of course, like most words in the English language, "fun" is in the eyes of the beholder.

Not everybody is meant to be an entrepreneur, but in all likelihood if you're reading these words—*you* are! That means you know the joys, the heartaches, the exhilaration and the indigestion of starting your own company.

CHARACTERISTICS OF A START-UP (LEVEL 1) COMPANY

Every start-up is unique. From market niche to office decor to staff (if any), there are as many variations as there are entrepreneurs.

However, I've consistently noticed that nearly all start-ups share these nine characteristics:

1. *The founders are actively involved in running the company.* As companies grow and evolve, those who were

there at the beginning often ease their feet off the gas and
reluctantly or willingly hand the steering wheel to others.
On the contrary, you know you're at a start-up when
the founders are still at the center of everything. On any
given day, they might be making critical decisions about
the company logo, delivery processes, human resources
models, hiring and firing, even office supplies. And
unlike the regular employees of emerging and dominating
companies, the rank and file of the start-up company still
have direct and daily access to the founders. Often, the
very atmosphere at a start-up is charged with the founder's
enthusiasm and philosophy, making things like vision and
mission statements living, evolving things.

2. *The founders are technically oriented experts, product
   gurus or market builders—and usually not skilled
   managers.* Where is it written that skillful entrepreneurs
   are also skillful leaders or managers? In fact, the opposite
   is often true. Likewise, an idea person isn't always a people
   person but may believe that his or her creation is brilliant
   enough to weather any management or moral issue. *This is
   the Achilles' heel of most successful startups: The all-stars
   who put you on the map are not always the champions
   who will help you grow.* To ensure true growth—and
   not just increased customer orders or profits—you need
   a management team capable of developing high-potential
   people.

3. *The primary emphasis is on producing products or
   services and selling them.* While it may not seem like it at
   first blush, a start-up is actually a rather simple creature,
   born, bred and nourished for one thing—to produce
   products (or services) and sell them. The partnerships,
   the charities, the bowling leagues, the rights and
   responsibilities of a mature company, all come later. For

now, it's all about production and sales. Build and sell, sell and build!

4. *Management, processes and planning receive minimal emphasis.* In this phase of the Business Growth Cycle, the pace is fast and problems are solved on a first-come, first-served basis. Management philosophies, processes and planning receive little, if any, emphasis, given the lack of manpower and time. The problem with this is that when growth does occur, there is little to no superstructure in place to handle it. Growth just means that everyone works harder, longer.

5. *Communication is informal.* Informal communication can be a beast or a boon, depending on who's doing the communicating! With only a vague chain of command and few formal procedures for proposing strategies or filing complaints, it's up to management, if they don't want to be caught off guard, to learn the company scuttlebutt through whatever means are available. This type of communication system—or lack thereof—is rife with problems and ripe for abuse. Like a life-or-death game of telephone, what's said in one department often morphs into something else entirely before it reaches the leader's ears.

6. *Employees work long hours and are paid modest salaries.* The passion of a start-up is often the fuel that fills its employees' bellies, in lieu of leisure time and disposable income. Many employees sign on to be a part of something bigger than themselves, to get in on the ground floor of a golden opportunity or, for the more mercenary among them, to forgo big profits now for bigger rewards later. While this structure can work well for a while, many leaders fail to take into consideration that passion fills only the *emotional* fuel tank, not the *literal* one. Pay structures and compensation packages must evolve along with the

company if you want to avoid hard feelings and decreased production when you need it the most—as a Level 2 company.

7. *Management reacts more to customer needs than to team member needs.* Because a start-up constantly needs new customers to feed the beast, it quickly and almost uniformly adopts a profit-over-personnel structure that many companies never quite give up. In the beginning, it's sheer survival: Customers add to the profit; personnel decrease it. Some leaders will add personnel only if a lack of manpower is affecting production, while being more than happy to work existing employees for longer hours for the same pay if production doesn't dip.

8. *The company culture—the nonnegotiable values that dictate how to treat customers and one another—is generally understood and does not require a lot of reinforcement.* With so little distance between the corner office and the production floor, the culture of the average start-up company is usually pretty easy to decipher. It might be the subtle signs of a casual workplace, where everyone from the CEO to the intern dresses in jeans and T-shirts, or the more subtle importance of using organic produce in the lunchroom or recyclable packing material in the plant. While this system may work well for a small start-up, as growth occurs, the original participants move up—or on—leaving new hires to guess at company policy or philosophy if it is not clearly explained and lived daily.

9. *The growth is usually slow to moderate.* While every start-up might aspire to become the next Netflix or Facebook overnight, the reality is strikingly different. In fact, while growth for many start-ups is greater than the rate of inflation, it is usually slow to moderate.

Chances are, either you're here now or you've recently been here. That's because every start-up goes through these challenges, like a baby learning to walk. It's only through trial, error and more trial and error that real development happens.

GROWING PAINS

So your company is growing, and sure, you may feel *some* of these growing pains, but mentally you're already on to the future, focusing on the next big thing. Maybe you're developing precise market projections or investing hand over fist in salespeople to increase revenues quickly.

Hold up for a minute, because this is where, time and again, leadership and companies falter. Why? Because while you're focusing far into the horizon, there's a fire in the trash can at your feet. That's right, you're overlooking the overly obvious and embarrassingly simple repairs you need to make in order to mature and stabilize. It's like adding a wing to your house before you finish the original roof. You're setting yourself up for hardship and struggle.

Often the very things that make a start-up so lean, mean and able to succeed—simple management structure, rapid-fire communication, charismatic leadership, passionate employees, a laser focus on growth—are the very things that turn growth into a stumbling block or even a crisis. Why? Because you're too focused on the next thing, and the next thing after that.

Lack of foresight is a *huge* issue for start-up leaders. They are so focused on growing revenues that they spend little to no time actually *preparing* for growth in any real and actionable way. So when it happens, the existing structures are easily overwhelmed and those informal hallway meetings often become shouting matches.

This is the key difference between simply growing a business, via increased sales or additional employees, and actually *scaling* a business for success.

Growing a business uses "see and solve" strategies. Scaling a business uses "predict and prepare" strategies. Growing a business may get you to the top; scaling a business gets you *and* keeps you there.

I often refer to this first inflection point, between a Level 1/Start-up business and a Level 2/Hyper-Growth business, as "growing pains." To avoid a crisis at this inflection point, two things need to be addressed: leadership and systems/processes. If these two critical issues are not addressed, they will eventually derail the company's ability to scale. Let's take a closer look at some common forms these "growing pains" take.

PROBLEM AREAS FOR LEVEL 1 COMPANIES

Here are pitfalls I've seen time and again in the start-up phase.

- *When there are two or more founders or partners in the business, it is not clear who is in charge and where accountability lies.* Often when you walk into a company mail room you'll see three or four boxes on the top, all leaders/founders sharing responsibility in a slightly squishy, feel-good leadership scenario where they all play hot potato with the big issues, rarely making fast, efficient or even wise decisions. As I like to tell such companies, "You can't hunt like a cheetah if you've got the organizational structure of a jellyfish!" At the end of the day, the buck must stop somewhere. And it should only truly stop once.
- *There are unresolved issues.* Conflicts between founders or partners, some dating back to when the company was

just an idea, may remain unresolved. With more than one ego involved, or a democratic structure dependent on total consensus or voting, it's a miracle anything gets done. Just take a look at Congress!

- *Leadership has difficulty setting priorities.* Often, newer employees are less motivated by dedication to the company's guiding principles, values and visions and more motivated by the conventional rewards of money and status. They weren't there at the very beginning; they're not as emotionally invested as the founders. It's important that the entire team focuses on the right things, together.

- *Financial controls are inadequate.* During the start-up phase, budgeting and cash control are often insufficient. Maybe the CEO or a family member has been trying to keep the books, or there are too many company credit cards floating around. Who's keeping an eye on the balance sheet? Who really knows the cause-and-effect relationships among cash flow, balance sheet, owner's equity and the profit-and-loss statement, and who can deploy and manage these resources to get predetermined outcomes?

- *Cash flow is low.* Budget constraints, poor planning or misuse of cash leads to working capital shortages. With the right skills and experience, this can be avoided. But do you have them in your early start-up? Most start-ups focus on hiring salespeople before they seek out a financial whiz.

- *Financial reporting is often slow and inaccurate.* What's more, the use of key performance data is not sufficient to predict problems and develop necessary coping strategies. You really need that finance guy in place, pronto!

- *Entrepreneurial founders are often tempted to diversify into unrelated products, services or businesses.* This is a biggie! I once consulted for a company that specialized in a highly technical field: creating the "clean room" technology needed to house super compressor computers. Then one day, one of the leaders decided he had cracked the code on how to be successful in anything and decided to invest in . . . a trailer park. Dealing with the fallout from an unwise—and unrelated—diversification product nearly bankrupted the company and certainly derailed its success for a number of years. Think about all the abandoned distractions in your start-up. You must stay focused on what's truly important.

Happily, all these issues can be prevented by paying a little attention to the two key factors mentioned earlier: leadership and processes.

Leaders who are very technical or market driven—however charismatic—can be a liability to a company focused on growth. The first step is recognizing these weaknesses, which is harder than it sounds. The founder may see herself as the personal embodiment of the company, so how could she *not* be the person to lead its growth?

The good news is, you most likely own all or part of the business, so you get to stay. But you must be honest about your strengths and weaknesses and build a team around you to complement your skills and compensate for your shortcomings.

Leaders must actively bolster or counteract these limitations to achieve growth. You need to build a strong leadership team. Again, this is easier said than done. Hiring is inherently difficult, and leaders make it worse, either consciously or subconsciously, by being afraid to hire people who may be smarter than they are. You must learn to hire for growth, to address the critical issues of process and systems that will enable this growth.

For perhaps the first time, you'll realize there is a stark difference between having the title of a leader and actually being a leader. The first step may need to be admitting you do not know exactly what leadership means or looks like and that you're out of your comfort zone. The best leaders examine what real leadership looks like in their business, but most leaders just try to fake it until they make it. They end up as skeletons on the side of Everest. You'll see them on your summit to the top, so take heed now.

The problem for most start-ups is that they got into business to sell a product or service. It wasn't easy, but it was very simple—and it's in their technical comfort zone: "I have this widget, technology, pet rock, skateboard or software to sell and I need someone to help me sell it." At the inflection point between a Level 1 and Level 2 company, entrepreneurs must realize that why they *started* the business no longer matters; they are now in the business of . . . *growing* a business.

These are two very different things, and they take two very, very different skill sets. Chances are good that the person or people who started the company aren't always the ones who can effectively grow it without a mentor who has climbed this same mountain. Not a mentor who has read about it, dreamed about it, developed mind-numbing, idealistic theories and stories on how it should be done, but someone who can climb out of the generalities and help you predict the details of your journey.

We all know how painful—and personal—making leadership changes can be. But again, it's critical to get the right people in the right places *at the right time.* The right time is not after a crisis but before a crisis occurs. This is one of the gut wrenching and therefore difficult decisions a leader has to make. Don't worry; we go in-depth on this critical topic in the first warning sign of success, Right Idea, Wrong Person (see chapter 7).

Processes and systems are the other keys to growing from Level 1 to Level 2. If you don't design your processes for growth, growth simply can't occur. It's like expecting your child to wear the same shoes on his seventh birthday that he wore on his third. Processes create predictable outcomes. And if you don't intentionally design the processes, they will design themselves. In other words, if you accept the possibility of chaos and hire just for production rather than choose experienced and proven managers who can build for future growth, new employees will simply perpetuate the current reality rather than approach the future with clarity. Short-term solutions, never intended to be permanent, will become permanent, no matter how awkward or inefficient.

I often hear business leaders say, "We're so busy working *in* the business that we don't have time to work *on* the business." Unfortunately, if you can't find a way to do both, there may not be a business to work *in or on* much longer.

Building processes and systems excites some people and bores others to tears. But it's like building the foundation of a house. You can't lay your Italian marble tile directly on the dirt; it'll never, ever look or work right.

And process changes can be hard to implement, especially if your employees have always done it one way. At the beginning, the new process feels inefficient, and maybe it is. You may need to try several methods before hitting on the right one. It can take time, but let me tell you, it's worth it.

I once worked with a company that for years had spent money hand over fist on marketing, but they could never really tie their efforts directly to closed deals. So, several years into the company's history, metrics became mandatory, and the right leader—someone who had set up a demand generation system for much larger organizations—stepped in to get it set up. It took months, integration of software programs, "data guys" working with "creative marketing types," staying in the conversation even when they did not *feel* like it and the sales team was skeptical. Most of the time, it was no fun.

But finally, a few months in, they could see which marketing dollars were actually resulting in closed deals. Marketing and sales worked closely together to tighten their target audience to deliver only the best leads. The data guys created meaningful reports based on accurate, relevant data that all the teams could use to manage their businesses.

The right systems helped marketing and sales focus on what was really important. Now the marketing budget was spent with surety rather than guesswork, down to the smallest details of each campaign.

Changing leadership and processes is almost never fun. That's why many start-ups try to skip it—and usually pay the price. But if you get this part right, you're perfectly set up for Level 2.

Then it gets fun again.

FOUR

LEVEL 2

HYPER-GROWTH

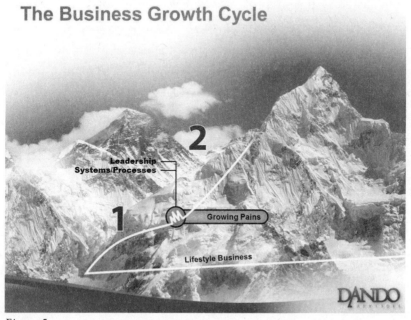

The Business Growth Cycle

Leadership
Systems/Processes

2

1

Growing Pains

Lifestyle Business

DANDO

Figure 5

THE START OF LEVEL 2 IS ANOTHER EXCITING TIME. REMEMBER, each phase begins with steady growth and stability and ends with significant organizational turmoil. During Level 2, sales are coming in faster and faster, often beating forecasts. Your team works long hours for modest wages, hoping to create a future of personal wealth and financial freedom.

Growth is rapid, sometimes exponential, with no end in sight. It's easy to think you've cracked the code on how to really grow a business. But watch out! Don't let rebellion rear its overly confident head again.

I'm hoping that you and your leadership team have addressed the Level 1 inflection points before reaching Level 2, but I also know that, if there is a very strong market for your products or services, you can "brute force" your way to this stage with the same leadership and processes you've always had. Of course, I don't recommend this (and maybe it's the very reason you're reading this book). This can create some severe unintended consequences that will bite you later in the Level 2/Hyper-Growth phase. But either way, you're here, so let's keep going.

Recognizing rapid growth as a two-sided coin doesn't make you a pessimist, just a realist—and realists are far more prepared to weather the storms ahead than rosy-eyed optimists, who wrongly assume that rapid growth is not only sustainable, but inevitable and smooth. The truth is, sometimes things have to get *worse* so they can get *better*.

For example, we don't want to have to report that we need to reduce profits so we can take time to fire brilliant jerks or implement new structures that will take time to have a positive impact. Remember, there has *never* been a company whose growth has been smooth, linear or inevitable—yet you've likely never seen (much less shown) business projections that include a conscious plan to slow down first to speed up later. We only want to see charts go up and to the right; anything else is failure, pure and simple, right?

Wrong.

As I like to say, the truth will set you free (though it may make you mad at first). If you are not free, then you are not dealing with the truth or you're not applying it . . . the truth is the truth!

Once again, if you have been wildly successful, this phase comes to an end with severe organizational turmoil and you come to the next inflection point of growth. Yes, it is absolutely counterintuitive and frustrating, but it is also normal and true. It is the price of growth and success and it's worth it. I have termed this inflection point "the crisis" because you cannot force your way through this inflection point like you could between Level 1 and Level 2.

In fact, often the issues that needed to be addressed between Level 1 and Level 2 still have not been addressed and are now, unbeknownst to you, sowing the seeds of your decay. *Caution:* Only about 15% of companies make the transition from a Level 2 to a Level 3 business.

CHARACTERISTICS OF A HYPER-GROWTH (LEVEL 2) COMPANY

Here's what a Level 2 company actually looks like. What characteristics does your company have? Remember, there are many Level 2 companies that have not achieved all of these characteristics. That's fine for now, but it's a sure bet that you'll never grow to Level 3/Market Leader until you resolve them all.

1. *A capable leader is at the company helm.* By this
   juncture a company should have done away with multiple
   leaders or a "feel good" approach to leadership and
   instead designated a level-headed, capable leader and
   complementary leadership team to oversee growth.

2. *As growth occurs, the physical properties of the company grow in turn, literally expanding.* The business often has multiple locations, such as sales offices, branch offices and off-site warehouses.

3. *Your focus diversifies.* You pay more attention to functions outside production and sales, such as marketing, inventory management, team member benefits and development, budgeting, finance and process support.

4. *Employee jobs are more specialized.* Where you once had one person who ran sales and marketing, now there are separate departments with different leaders and expanded teams. Individuals do specific jobs, rather than "anything and everything."

5. *More is less (effective).* Frequently, the company becomes more impersonal, simply because there are more employees, more initiatives, more opportunities, more, more, more.

6. *The growth rate is faster than it was in Level 1.* In fact, sometimes it's much, much faster. Watch out: "Complexity creep" can take over as the old corporate culture (see the next point) clashes with the new, second-generation hires.

7. *The culture needs to be explicitly communicated.* Your company culture—the nonnegotiable values, performance expectations and ways of treating customers and one another—now needs to be communicated and reinforced in words and actions that match. Accountability cannot be sporadic or random. Remember, not everyone was here when the original values and performance expectations were set in stone. It takes a bit of conscious work to keep them alive and share them with new team members.

As successful companies grow, they often grow themselves into problems, but because they deal with them openly and honestly, they normalize the journey and keep growing. As unsuccessful companies grow, they also grow themselves into problems, but rather than tackling them head-on, they hide, isolate, ignore and often go out of business, either imploding or shrinking themselves out of the market.

The good news is that if you're still in business and you're experiencing problems, congratulations! You're a success. Patterns, history and experience show that every successful company matures into a predictable series of surmountable problems that are a direct result of their previous growth and success.

Don't let the fact that you are experiencing problems derail the success you're experiencing. Every successful company has problems, but those that surmount them both predict and deal with them. Sure, no one ever wants the problems, but they are as much a part of your success as oxygen is of life.

The unsuccessful company will either deny or ignore problems, assuming that more success, more employees or even more sales will make them go away. Successful companies that deal with and scale for growth will accept the problems and deal with them head-on, even predicting future problems to avoid. They'll build strong muscles that will translate into strong business practices.

Often one or more problems block a successful company's transition to a higher level of performance. If company leaders fail to predict and prevent these problems, the company will fight the same battles in precisely the same way, churning on and on, year after year, until—finally—although the business does not explode, the people often do.

When these crises emerge, it is what a company does in response that determines if it moves on and becomes a Level 3/ Market Leader, or if it simply moves on aimlessly—or worse.

The Level 2/Hyper-Growth phase is such a double-edged sword that I'm surprised I don't cut myself just talking about it! Let's look at some of the most common problems of this stage.

When growth occurs, often because of a good product, a good sales team, a healthy market or all of the above, you can begin to think that you are invincible, that all those press clippings and magazine features are accurate. In short, you can begin to think that you can do no wrong. And, as I like to say, nothing kills faster than success. The rebellion phase is in full swing.

PROBLEM AREAS FOR LEVEL 2 COMPANIES

If these problems are present, they will eventually derail your company's ability to scale. It is the role of you, the leader, and your leadership team to *predict and resolve* these problems *before* they show up in the results:

- *There's misalignment at the top.* The executive leadership team does not function as an aligned team:
  - They may all nod their heads and even say things like "we have to all stack hands on this," but once they leave the room their actions tell a different story.
  - Entitlement or arrogance plagues one or more of the executive team members, who were once all-stars but have become troublemakers or brilliant jerks.
  - There are some long-term loyal employees or recent hires on the executive team who have not or cannot develop their managerial skills to meet the needs of the business.
  - Friction emerges between old and new executive team members, and infighting ensues. It becomes more about "us versus them" than "all together now."

- *Mismanagement seeps through the organization.* The company starts feeling the effects of not being run by a qualified and experienced management team.
  - Your top performers are brought together to become the management team. However, this group has little *experience* working as a team and lacks the *expertise* necessary to scale a business by *predicting and preparing* for the problems *before* they show up in the results. If they have never functioned at this level of leadership before, it's highly unlikely they can be successful in the face of the inevitable crises that all successful companies eventually face.
  - Delegation becomes increasingly difficult for the CEO and other managers. I was talking with a CEO just the other day who told me, "I have asked Luke at least four times to get his final product road map to me. He keeps giving me generalities and multiple ideas but nothing that directly connects to our 2014 goal. . . . I am starting to wonder if he is the wrong guy, and I think I may have to jump in and get it done myself." What he was really thinking, but not saying (another one of those sweet little lies that leaders tell themselves so they do not have to face the issue head-on), was that he had asked multiple times, thought he was clear on what he wanted, and cannot believe he is not getting something so simple. He's feeling a bit of disbelief that Luke, his VP of product, is so disrespectful that he hasn't given him what he wanted, when he wanted it. I asked him whether he thought that if I asked Luke to give me the details of what this CEO wanted and by when, Luke could clearly communicate the expectations and know how to deliver. The CEO said,

"I sure hope so. After all, he *is* my VP of product." I
told him that delegation is one of the hardest things
a leader has to do, and what's more, it does not come
naturally to most. I told him that delegation is not
dumping the stuff you do not like to do, or the stuff
you ran out of time to do, or the stuff that you used to
do but do not want to do anymore. I went on to talk
to him about the three basic reasons people do not do
something they're asked to do:

1. They do not know *how*. Whose responsibility is
   that? It is your responsibility to teach them before
   you delegate to them. They have to prove they
   know *how* before you can fully delegate.

2. They *cannot* do what you are asking them to do.
   Not everyone can do everything. I cannot dunk
   a basketball; therefore, if my job required me to
   dunk a basketball, I would be in trouble. You could
   send me to all kinds of classes on how to dunk a
   basketball, get me the best coaches in the world,
   but at the end of the day, I cannot dunk. If you are
   asking someone to do something they cannot do
   and you have put them in a position where their
   paycheck and employment depend on their doing
   it, then they will go to the classes and try extra-
   hard, but at the end of the day, they still cannot
   do it. Whose responsibility is it if someone is in a
   position for which they *cannot* do the work? Right
   again: yours! Do not do that to someone; it is
   mean!

3. They *won't* do it. They have proven they are
   capable and, in fact, they have done what you have
   asked them to do perfectly in the past, but now,

for whatever reason, they do not like doing it, it is hard, they think they are above the task, and so on, so they *won't* do the work, and they hold you hostage. If someone *won't* do the work, whose responsibility is it? Very good. Do you see the pattern of who is at the core of why delegation does or does not work? It is *you!*

- *Access to the CEO becomes rare for managers and employees.* As a result, line managers feel better qualified than the CEO or other executives to make decisions in their technical areas, but they are not permitted to make them. This stifles ingenuity and creativity, not just from them but from the entire organization.

- *Senior management feels it is losing control due to less direct contact with day-to-day operations.* You start to see and hear a lot more about "us versus them" throughout the business, not just on the executive team. People take sides in an effort to protect, or at least insulate, themselves, again shutting off the entire organization from the cooperation, teamwork and creativity it will need to survive, let alone thrive.

- *There's a need for constant monitoring at the top.* At this rapid state of growth, the need for leaders is greater than the time required to groom them. Gradually, or not so gradually in some cases, it becomes apparent that some of the senior management team members are not developing as skilled leaders or executives.

- *There's a shift in balance.* One or a few customers or products represent a disproportionate amount of the company's business, so there's increased vulnerability to competition. Remember my earlier story about the printing company that had one major client they never thought they'd lose, so they ignored any other attempts to court new customers or prepare for a day when they might not have that client around anymore? That's a great example of this "shift in balance" that we're talking about here.

- *The company begins compromising on quality for the sake of rapid growth.* If you're not careful—and a lot of companies aren't—customer centricity begins to disintegrate at this stage. The perception is that you're growing so fast, you don't need to focus on quality. After all, it's certainly not hurting your success. But just like busy restaurants that ignore their regular customers in favor of big parties of spring breakers or winter tourists, the day will come when that growth levels off, and if you've burned enough bridges with your loyal customers, then where will you be?

- *The pace of execution slows.* While growth is brisk, the response to growth is sluggish—or worse, nonexistent. Your executive leadership team is slow to react to or does not understand changing market conditions and increasing competition. Meanwhile, those on the front lines, who are seeing the rapid pace of change firsthand, grow frustrated with management's unresponsiveness, sometimes frustrated enough to leave.

- *There are often increased internal problems that threaten the company's ability to scale.* All companies struggle from within, but growth shines the spotlight on a lot of these troubles, for example:
  - Infighting among managers and supervisors
  - Outdated corporate cultures
  - "Look the other way" deals on nonnegotiable values for certain "special" employees who are considered invaluable and thus above—or outside—the rules
  - Inefficient or outdated systems and processes that threaten growth from the ground up

- Bureaucracy that becomes so impenetrable that nothing, or close to nothing, gets done

- *Poor decisions + poor decision makers = poor results.* Poor decisions are one thing, and poor decision makers are another. Both are crippling to growth, but together they are a real handicap. Results that *look like success* often *breed failure* due to poor decision making by unqualified managers in the following areas:
  - Systems design and improvement
  - Facilities expansion and purchase
  - Recruiting and hiring key employees
  - Using cash
  - Commitment to new products or services

- *Accountability becomes confused and sporadic.* With growth comes the need for more accountability, not less. But with so many new people to blame, the blame becomes more rich and multilayered and, of course, more common.

- *Meetings become awkward.* Problem-predicting and problem-solving meetings and processes can be awkward, time-consuming and, at times, ineffective. Sometimes lower-level team members don't feel they can openly question top leadership's actions because of this "us versus them" divide, putting you at more risk when you cancel out the power of what they might have had to say. These missed opportunities may become near-daily events.

- *Mixed money messages.* The company has areas of tight and loose cost controls, so team members are unsure of how to spend money.

- *There are major shortages of management time and cash.* I worked with a company, often featured on top magazine covers and referred to widely as the "darling" of the industry, that was facing a $250,000 tax bill and in danger of losing the company to the IRS. Time was running out, so they called me in. After ramping up, I realized the company was sitting on a massive inventory gathering dust in a huge warehouse. They had bought tons of equipment, gadgets, bells and whistles to help them run or grow their company but hadn't yet implemented them. And they were in no danger of doing so anytime soon, particularly if they went out of business. We had a huge fire sale and made more than enough to cover the tax bill, then helped the company get back on its feet with more realistic growth and budgetary expectations. Again, it comes down to taking a step back and seeing the solution from a different angle. It was hard to believe this group of smart executives couldn't see the answer sitting right under their noses, but we all do it.

- *Vendor relationships become strained.* Long-term service providers are no longer able—or willing—to effectively serve the company as a result of the mixed messages that may mean deferred, or no, payment.

- *Politics abound.* Throughout the company, hiring friends, family members or well-known corporate "heroes" becomes more important than getting qualified people in key positions and clearly defining and enforcing accountability. Sacred cows destroy the ability to be honest about people's performance; employees' performance becomes more about the alliances they create with people at the top. The company becomes a political beast.

- *Systems and reporting don't meet increased demand.* Financial performance reporting and control systems are often inadequate for sales volume. New leaders want data sliced and diced differently, but the team can't get there with the current systems.

- *"Don't let the door hit you . . ."* Thanks to the internal chaos and decrease in employee morale and customer service, key employees become disenchanted and leave. While you may assume there is an infinite talent pool eager to get in your door, industry circles are small, and once the word is out that your company is an unstable, or even unpleasant, place to work, the best recruits will no longer be knocking quite so loudly.

The inflection point between a Level 2/Hyper-Growth company and a Level 3/Market Leader is often marked by one consistent similarity: *crisis*. We cannot "brute force" our way from a Level 2 to a Level 3 company. It takes brains over brawn—and it's often much, much more difficult to use your brain.

Much as we had two critical issues to address between Level 1 and Level 2, here we have three items to address:

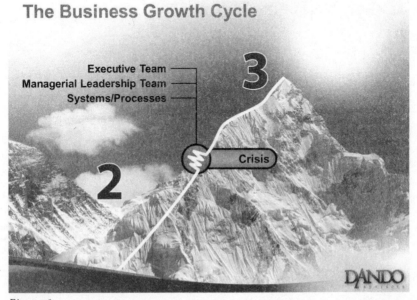

The Business Growth Cycle

Executive Team
Managerial Leadership Team
Systems/Processes

3

2

Crisis

DANDO

Figure 6

1. *Executive team alignment.* To properly transition to
   Level 3/Market Leader, you must have an executive team
   that *trusts one another,* is aligned and is focused on
   achievable goals. You need a leader who can passionately
   and clearly say, "Here is our company, North Star. Here
   is where we're going, here is how we're going to get there
   and, most importantly, here is *why.*" Unfortunately,
   what often happens during the Hyper-Growth phase is
   that the executive team comes together accidentally, not
   deliberately as a result of a specific purpose and vision.
   Scattered focus equals scattered results. Alternatively,
   aligned focus equals game-changing results. An aligned
   leadership team will always outperform and move
   faster than a scattered focus team. It is hard to see with
   the naked eye but the illustration below highlights the
   difference.

Executive Team

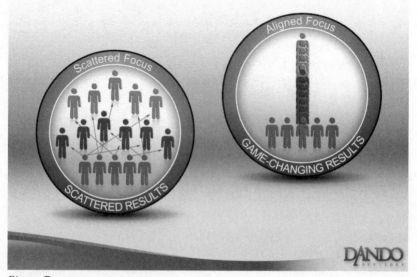

Figure 7

2. *Managerial team strength.* Perception and reality are frequently at odds in fast-growing organizations. Often, the official organizational structure bears no resemblance to how business is actually done. For example, your organizational chart may show clearly defined sales, finance and operations teams, with leaders who report to the CEO. This may be fine for a small organization, but in a growing one, it's important that the department leaders are able to actually lead their teams. If, in reality, all decisions must ultimately go through the CEO, it creates a bottleneck that is guaranteed to slow growth and stunt leadership development at the departmental level. Many organizations "solve" this problem by bringing in a president to act as a go-between from the departments to the CEO. This person usually has no real authority; he's just a mouthpiece. The bottleneck remains, and everyone hates the new mouthpiece. Talk about a no-win situation!

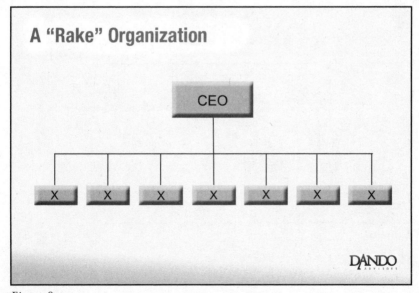

Figure 8

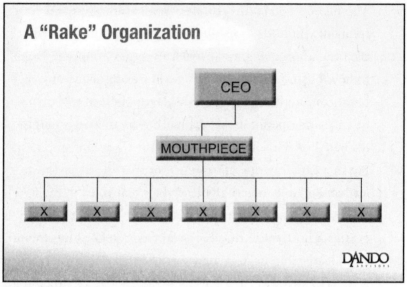

Figure 9

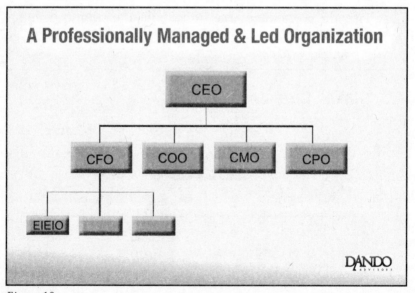

Figure 10

Whatever structure ultimately works for you and your company, it must be customer-centric, support the weight of growth and realistically evolve with the business. No fixed structure will work the same for every company. Often, leaders recruited from other companies will come in and try to force an organizational structure that's simply not appropriate.

3. *Systems and processes falter.* Often the systems and processes that worked for a start-up can't scale with rapid growth, and they most definitely won't work for a Level 3/Market Leader. One company I worked for grew because it had multiple offices run by invested owners who had a clear passion and focus for the company's success. This made them very versatile, adaptable, accessible and ultimately successful—as a start-up. But when rapid growth came on, the manager/owners of the field offices were unable to scale. They became rigid, institutionalized and isolated; they basically worked for themselves. Rather than having a unified kingdom under one recognized leader, there were dozens of tiny fiefdoms unto themselves.

We often miss the warning signs of success, not because we're not looking for them or even aware of them, but because the truth really, really hurts. It's much easier to bury our heads in our day-to-day business dealings and ignore the harsh truths of the problems that lurk around the corner—and often under our own noses.

Hearing that the systems and processes you have in place are not working—and not sustainable for growth—is like hearing you're flying at 30,000 feet, the engines on your plane won't get you to your destination and now you must go out on the wing and change the engines, hoping you don't crash, burn and die first. The task feels, in a word, insurmountable.

The Business Growth Cycle

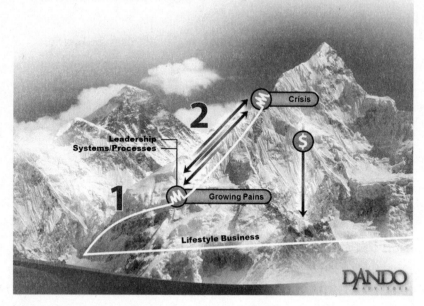

Figure 11

At this crisis point in the Business Growth Cycle, there are typically four things that can happen, and three of them are not good. (Can you guess which?)

1. *Shrink.* Go back and get smaller, either because you lost customers or because you could not handle the weight of growth. You may be able to fix some things, like updating your processes (e.g., cash-flow projections, cost tracking, customer service, etc.) or getting the right people in and the wrong people out. Then you grow again until you hit this crisis inflection point again, and then go back and get smaller, fix some things (perhaps *really* emphasize accountability), then get bigger, hit this inflection point again, go back and get smaller, fix some other things . . .

You get the point. This isn't necessarily a death sentence, but it is an emotional roller coaster and inevitably leads to the next point.

2. *Experience "Groundhog Day."* You keep fighting the same or slightly different battles the same way, day after day, month after month, until, if the business doesn't explode, the people do . . . often at one another. People lose sight of everything else due to frustration.

3. *Cash flow yourself out of business.* At this inflection point between Level 2 and Level 3, there are a lot of profitable businesses that cash flow themselves out of business . . . really! See the tenth and twelfth warning signs of success, False Security of Revenues and Sowing the Seeds of Decay, to understand how this could happen.

4. *Become a market leader.* You deal directly, honestly and boldly with the three critical issues identified between Level 2 and Level 3 and become one of the rare leaders and companies to mature into Level 3 and become a market leader as I have defined it.

THREADING THE NEEDLE

There is a moment during the Hyper-Growth phase where revenues are climbing but expenses start to creep up as well, and we start to see more customer churn than we expect or want. In every high-growth business, expenses eventually catch up to revenues. But it's critical to keep an eye on expenses to avoid disaster.

When expenses meet or overtake revenues, I call it "threading the eye of the needle." And it's never, ever fun. You will read about this again in the tenth Warning Sign of Success: the False Security of Revenues.

Figure 12 shows how threading the eye of the needle occurs at this intersection where profit and expenses inevitably meet.

Overcoming this crisis takes sharp attention to detail and all hands on deck. You may need to make dramatic changes to get through this, and it's a problem that cannot be ignored (though, of course, it could have been predicted).

How a company deals with this is often indicative of how it deals with any crisis. Rigid, inflexible companies have a tendency to implode. But flexible companies that are open to change and new ideas use it as an opportunity to learn.

Because it's such a loaded moment, it makes your company an easy mark for outsiders seeking takeover. From their perspective, small changes—maybe a reduction in personnel or a quick cash infusion—are easy to make. They prey on your vulnerability to

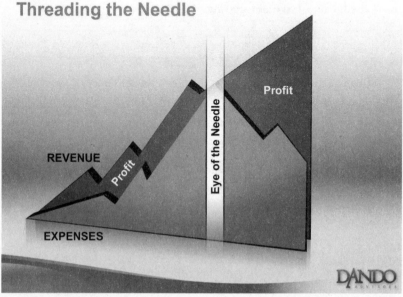

Figure 12

take your company for a good price. You may acquiesce simply to feel the relief that comes with escaping tough decisions.

Then the new owners come in and do exactly what you could have done yourself, keeping your business intact to grow even larger! They'll consider the executive leadership team, perhaps replacing some members with more tenured executives. They'll find or train competent, experienced managers. They'll put predictable processes and systems in place that help them overcome this crisis and build on the company's original success. They will take it through the eye of the needle and get the fruits on the other side.

Again, you can do all this yourself. Why not do the hard work now to experience the great potential upswing on the other side?

These are precisely the three things that must be addressed in order to move from a Level 2 organization to a Level 3. You can do it, or you can hand the reins to someone else. But this work must get done for the company to become a market leader. There is no way around it.

These three, clearly defined issues are based on the wisdom of professionals who have successfully scaled, matured and stabilized organizations. Don't believe for a minute that you can't do this, too. You can. And you will, if you want to make it to your market leadership goal.

Think about it: See your company or department through the eyes of someone considering taking it over. You already know the three things any "new" owner would address to "fix" your business. You can just as easily do these yourself:

1. Address issues on the executive leadership team.
2. Improve your managerial leadership team.
3. Create predictable, scalable systems and processes.
   (See figure 4 in chapter 3.)

All you need to do is put yourself in their shoes: Analyze your situation from an outside perspective. Of course, that's easier said than done. The reason takeover teams can quickly assess the current warning signs and quickly eradicate them to either grow or sell is precisely because they are objective. They're not emotionally invested in whether you succeed or fail, as long as they profit.

You, on the other hand, probably started this company with the very people you now need to reprimand or eradicate. While no one is suggesting you become a dictator or tyrant, you can't be blindly loyal to one or two people at the expense of dozens or hundreds of people who might lose their jobs if you fail. It isn't just bad business; it's bad decision making—not to mention borderline immoral.

Threading the eye of the needle is a critical juncture, a watershed moment, a tipping point that needs to be addressed if you are to see the light at the end of the tunnel.

Phase 2 comes to an end with sometimes severe organizational turmoil in the face of this crisis, but it leads us to the next inflection point of growth. Phase 2 always ends in a crisis, because you cannot "brute force" your way through the inflection point between Level 2 and Level 3 like you could between Level 1 and Level 2. You absolutely must use your brainpower and leadership to solve this crisis.

It's where you prove that you have the leadership team, managers and processes in place to become a market leader. Without all three, you can never make it.

FIVE

LEVEL 3

MARKET LEADER

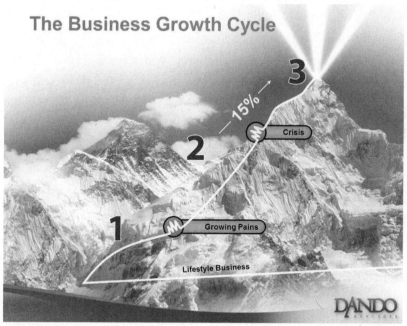

The Business Growth Cycle

1 Growing Pains
Lifestyle Business
2
— 15% →
Crisis
3

DANDO

Figure 13

CONGRATULATIONS! YOU HAVE NAVIGATED YOUR WAY THROUGH the crisis that brought you to Level 3! Only about 15% of companies become a Level 3 business, a market leader. Obviously, the climb is never over. But you've navigated through what causes approximately 85% of leaders and their businesses to fail—or at least fall short of their financial or emotional expectations.

As I stated earlier, the Business Growth Cycle is an *approximation* of how a business grows. Every business has its own unique journey; you know your industry and your business best. Every business and its component parts are at different stages of growth (if you acquire another business and stitch it into your business or start a new division in another location, it may be a Level 1 or Level 2 business, while your primary business is operating as a Level 3 business). Your awareness of these shifting dynamics will profoundly impact how you resource, handle and grow that business inside of your business.

By becoming a Level 3 business, you have significantly increased your strategic opportunities to scale yourself, your team, your business, your financial freedom and your influence to change the world.

Typically, you are now widely recognized, internationally, nationally or locally, as the market leader. You may be the Nike, Apple or Microsoft of recycled nursery products, organic sports drinks or handmade Christmas ornaments. But getting to the top is only half the battle; now the real work of *staying* at the top begins. As you may imagine, it requires a completely new, unique skill set to manage this phase of the Business Growth Cycle.

CHARACTERISTICS OF A MARKET LEADER (LEVEL 3) COMPANY

As one might suspect, market leaders are in a distinct class all by themselves. This is what a market leader looks like:

1. *Settling down and settling in.* The organization is at
   a place where problem predicting gets more focus and
   reward than problem solving. As a result, aligned executive
   and middle management teams are in place and are staffed
   with qualified people, and *accountability is clear* and well
   managed. As a result, your Level 2 crisis is resolved.

2. *Narrowing the focus.* You have analyzed the market
   and your place in it. With that perspective in place, the
   company's business niche is clearly defined and its products
   and services fit the niche. Growth may have leveled out
   but is still sustainable because it is controlled and, what's
   more, clearly understood.

3. *Coming into its own.* As the organization continues to
   grow and evolve, it begins to take on an identity beyond
   the founders' and CEO's identities. This "new" identity
   allows for other players to participate and for many more
   voices to be heard.

4. *Staying goal oriented.* The company has well-defined and
   well-communicated short-term and intermediate-term
   strategies and plans, designed to reach specific, reasonable,
   measurable goals.

5. *Doing more managing (working "on" the business) than
   technical work (working "in" the business).* Managerial
   leaders are in place and are focused on developing systems,
   accountability and people that will enable the business to
   scale.

6. *Weeding out the unproductive.* Unproductive or
   unprofitable products and services are being phased out,
   gradually and with purpose. Focus is the name of the
   game, and that laser-like focus is allowing for growth
   that is organic and specific to the new market niche the
   organization has identified and chosen to follow.

7. *Employing timely and competent market research, development and planning.* There is no more "accidental" or "hopeful" growth, as fun and exciting as that can be. Instead, growth is dependent on timely, competent market research, development and planning. This prevails in all areas of the business, including products, services, customer care and acquisition, geographic coverage and competition.

8. *Utilizing competent staff, management and leadership development processes.* People development is a priority, hiring is fluid and recognition is important. Healthy debates are normal and opinions are heard. The result is leadership, management and staff that are competent and co-creative. These processes include regular performance feedback, training and ongoing coaching.

9. *Definitive decision making based on data.* Guesswork has been largely eliminated from the organization, leaving behind fact instead of fiction. Now managers effectively use financial and nonfinancial performance data in presenting, planning, decision making, problem predicting and expense control.

10. *Strong profitability.* The company's financial health is strong and cash flow works well.

BENEFITS OF BECOMING A LEVEL 3 BUSINESS

While the benefits of becoming a true market leader should be fairly obvious, here are some specific benefits you can expect from this level of business growth:

- *The sum becomes bigger than its parts.* The survival and continued development of the company are not dependent on one or just a few people. What's more, they're not dependent on one or two products or services. The goal is to be led by the organization rather than through a cult of personality or politics.

- *There is a future for the company.* Profitable growth and a long future are more assured at this level. Strategy and succession planning become priorities.

- *People are taking notice.* As a result of your past success, you can hire and retain more capable executive, management and technical employees. Gone are the days of bad word of mouth, and here are the days of your being a respected, sought-after company.

- *You have a strong managerial team.* When strong managerial leadership is in place, the organization is free to grow rather than simply exist. Delegation is fluid, expected and *effective*. This frees the owners and the C-suite to plan, pursue additional markets and react to major opportunities.

- *The company can grow bigger* and *better.* Thanks to the confidence and solidity of all of its levels—management, people, R & D, product, sales and the rest—the company can more effectively expand product lines and markets to ensure stable future growth.

- *Reaction times are quicker.* The company is able to quickly react to an adverse economy or market because it has the people and processes to be problem predictors rather than problem solvers!

- *Profitability is usually sustained.* Thanks to other factors firing on all cylinders, the organization finds it easier to make and sustain profits to keep the business running smoothly.

- *All employees gain increased energy and enjoyment.* Improved flexibility and stability usually make the business more enjoyable for the owners, managers and team members.
- *The owners can enjoy increased free time.* At last, the owners (mostly for closely held private companies) can spend more time away from the business . . . if they want. Most of us recognize the joy to be had in a good workday but also look forward to fewer of those days at some point. This is that point!
- *The company is priced to sell.* Thanks to all the preceding factors, the business is more marketable at a premium price should the owners want to sell or go public.
- *The company can capitalize on the success of others.* Such is the growth, and the stability of growth, as well as the free time of those in power, that acquisitions can be discussed. Smaller companies in the same industry can, and probably should, be successfully acquired. Many leaders try to do this as a response to the pain experienced in Level 2, but at that point it is a mistake. Focus and become a Level 3 company, and then start acquiring. Trust me—you will be happy you waited!

Every organization and its component parts are at different stages of development. These three levels—Level 1/Start-up, Level 2/Hyper-Growth and Level 3/Market Leader—are an *approximation* of what happens to *most* companies. They're not a precise measurement tool that lets you look at a calendar or check your watch and say, "Today I became a Hyper-Growth company! Nice!" If you do find your company at any of these levels, look at figure 4 in chapter 3 to help you guide your journey.

PART III

PROBLEM PREDICTING VS. PROBLEM SOLVING

THE 12 WARNING SIGNS OF SUCCESS— THE PREDICTIVE LEADER'S TOOL SET

DO YOU SOLVE PROBLEMS? OR DO YOU HEAD THEM OFF AT THE pass? On the surface, these might seem like the same question, but in fact there is a *profound, yet subtle, difference* between problem solving and problem predicting.

What's more, the way you succeed, grow, adapt and thrive as a company is *critically dependent* on how you answer the solve-versus-predict question.

PROBLEM SOLVING

Problem solving is taking action to make something *go away*. It is the action most rewarded and supported in business today. Heck, there are MBA-level courses taught on how to be a great problem solver. What no one ever tells you is that problem solving can actually *slow or kill* a business's ability to grow.

It may sound strange, but that behavioral muscle that you flex every time you're solving a problem—which grows stronger every time—is one of the main impediments to sustained growth and success in today's market.

The problem is systemic and often hard to spot, because the problem solvers often get all the recognition, pay increases and promotions.

This is only natural, since they are the ones staying late, helping lead the team through painful situations and showing a unique ability to think on their feet. Culturally, most businesses send the message that these are the actions of a star employee.

The unintended consequence is that we're developing and rewarding behaviors and habits that are valuable only in the face of crisis. When we reward those who solve problems, we overlook the much simpler—and far more valuable—skill of preventing problems in the first place. Remember, the goal is to *avoid* crises.

It is as obvious as it is logical: *People will do more of what is rewarded.* If you reward problem solving, people will *actively wait* until problems arise before they react. Why? Because that is the muscle memory that has been developed over time—mostly by accident.

And the "habit" of problem solving has one more pernicious, unacknowledged side effect—people get excited over actual problems. In some companies, problems are the *only* things anyone ever gets excited about. A secondary product of such companies becomes—you guessed it—problems.

In these situations, much of a company's resources, especially time, is spent solving problems instead of creating new products, revenue streams or customer pipelines.

Do you see the subtle but very destructive problem with problem solving?

THE PROBLEM WITH PROBLEM SOLVING

Problem solvers tend to propose elaborate schemes to define the problem, generate alternative solutions and put the best solutions into practice. Perhaps the most destructive problem of all is that problem solvers wait for problems to occur because they have been trained like Pavlov's dogs that the only way to be rewarded is to solve problems.

If this process is successful, you *might* eliminate the problem. Then what you have is the absence of the problem. But what you *do not* have is the presence of a result you want to create, or the exposure to and full possibilities of an opportunity to scale.

The path of least resistance in problem solving is to move from pain to relief and then from relief to pain again. This is because what drives action is the intensity of the problem or the pain: Remember what muscle memory you are building in your business; you get what you set yourself up for!

In problem solving, the focus isn't necessarily on *assessing risks and prioritizing the highest and best opportunities;* it's on the problem! This may be hard to see with the naked eye, but the consequences are not. Once the intensity of solving that problem is reduced, people have less motivation to act.

Thus, problem solving as a way of life not only becomes self-defeating but, unbeknownst to you and your employees, also builds muscle memory that actually atrophies the business's ability to grow.

PROBLEM PREDICTING

Problem predicting is taking action to head off conflicts before they show up in the results. Although your path to growth is likely unique to your market and industry, rapid growth tends to cause the same issues in every business. *The details may be different, but the dynamics are the same.* So there's no reason to waste brainpower solving issues that have already been solved in thousands of other companies. Instead, check the literature, and use your team's brainpower to innovate and create new products and services that allow your business to aggressively grow.

In this chaotic business environment, leaders must see around corners and *predict the problems* before they show up in the results. The good news is that you do not need a crystal ball to predict and prevent 90% of these problems. All you have to do is pay attention to the patterns, good and bad, and reward your problem predictors—*not* your problem solvers. *Remember: Success leaves footprints . . . and so does failure.*

So how do you achieve this shift? It's easy enough to spread the word that management is encouraging problem prevention. But your actions must back up your words. You must actively create teams or protocols to prevent problems. It takes a while to sink in, but once established in the culture, this change can yield big payoffs.

Keep reading. I am going to give you a lot of examples, stories, teachings and prescriptive advice on how to create this kind of culture in your organization.

Think about all the activity we create in the face of a crisis. For example, when your dog goes missing, you enlist the whole neighborhood to look for her; you put up signs, maybe even turn to a pet psychic. It completely upends your life. You can't focus on anything else until she comes home.

And then you notice the hole—or holes—in the fence. The ones that let her easily escape. Had you predicted the problem—kept up the maintenance on the fence—guess what? You wouldn't have to go through all the work to get your pet back. Think of all the time, resources, stress and energy you would have saved. What could you have used all that energy for instead? Wrote the great American novel? Planted a new flower bed? Started a dog-training school?

It's the same in business. Avoid the crises by predicting problems before they ever happen. It's overly obvious and embarrassingly simple.

But first, you must stop rewarding the behavior you do not want.

WHY PROBLEM PREDICTING IS OVERLY OBVIOUS AND EMBARRASSINGLY SIMPLE . . . BUT NEVER EASY

As an organization grows, it requires radically different leadership and management practices for the different stages of its growth. But that can be hard for entrenched leaders to see or admit. What should be a pure business concern becomes an emotional issue. Only a mature leader can predict this problem, communicate it to the team and set up systems to avoid this crisis (more on that in the 12 Warning Signs of Success; see chapters 7, 8 and 9).

Whether we've technically defined them or not, we all know business growth phases exist. You know, intellectually, that you won't always be a start-up, that you'll likely experience growth pains at some point and that if you do X, Y and Z you can eventually become a market leader. But *knowing* this and *doing* something about it are two different things.

My job is to help you see your company through my eyes, the eyes that have lived through building successful businesses and endured stressful, sleepless nights along the way. I get it; your business is your baby; you're too close to it and love it too much to see that it's—perhaps, just maybe—a little bit ugly.

I've done it countless times for leaders and their companies across all ranges of industries and revenues. What I notice every time is that if leadership could simply *step away* from the intrinsic and institutionalized problems that are present every day, the problem-solving culture would quickly become overly obvious and embarrassingly simple to them, too.

It's a little like walking into a moldy hotel room, one that just reeks with the moldy smell, even if you can't actually see the mold. The manager can't smell it, the housekeeper can't smell it, and maintenance can't smell it because they're in and out of that room all day long and have 1,001 different things on their minds. But *you* can smell it the moment you check in because your nose is new to the scene.

You can do this and I am going to show you how.

SIX

IS THERE A SERIAL KILLER AT WORK IN YOUR COMPANY?

Any intelligent fool can make things bigger, more complex, and more violent. It takes a touch of genius—and a lot of courage—to move in the opposite direction.

—Albert Einstein

IF YOU HAVE BEEN SUCCESSFUL IN BUSINESS, IT'S QUITE POSsible that a serial killer lurks somewhere in your company, strangling growth and destroying your chances of sustained profitability. It lives in the quagmire where simple goals turn into complicated plans because of cloudy expectations, vague accountability and a lack of leadership.

The killer's name is complexity, and it sneaks into an organization behind the mask of success. As I like to say, "Nothing kills faster than success."

The first step—and one of the hardest—in avoiding this killer is to identify where it resides in your company right now.

WHY IS COMPLEXITY SO SEDUCTIVE?

If something is complicated, it feels like harder work than is usually required has been done to "solve" the problem. As a result, complexity often conceals bad judgment, incompetence and inaction. It provides a perfect excuse for spinning your wheels, and while you'd never admit it, it can be a comfortable place to hide.

In a root-cause study performed by Bain & Company over a three-year period, the management consultant company asked 377 CEOs to disclose the primary barrier to achieving their goals, in essence, "What is the number one issue faced by CEOs?"[1] Executives reported that approximately 85% of the time their biggest obstacle was managing their time and energy in the face of growing complexity![2]

"IDEAS GONE WILD"

Humans are complex beings; we make even the most seemingly simple actions complex. Take relaxation, for example. I recently tried to have a "quiet" moment on a Saturday afternoon. All I wanted was to sit still, clear my mind and relax.

By the time I got to the point of taking a true break, I had filled my head with so much stuff about what I should be doing and should have done that I had fully complicated what was supposed to be a simple pause. While that may be a rudimentary example, it speaks volumes about how simple ideas easily go wild (even when we seek out just the opposite). This happens in businesses every day. I'll bet you are thinking of two or three examples yourself right now—how something so simple has turned into something so complicated.

WHY IS SUSTAINABLE GROWTH SO ELUSIVE?

The Bain & Company study also revealed a profound paradox. The company reviewed data from more than 8,000 companies the firm had worked with over the last 30 years and found that fewer than one in ten had achieved even a modest level of sustained, profitable growth over the past decade.[3]

In the same study, Bain & Company asked executives if they felt they had adequate opportunities in their market and industry to grow profitably. Guess what? Nine in ten said yes, they did have adequate opportunities for growth.[4]

So why did fewer than one in ten succeed in achieving the targets? (Hint: See CEOs' number one issue in the Bain & Company study, which CEOs said was managing their time and energy in the face of growing complexity.)

Are you starting to get the picture?

SO WHAT? NOW WHAT?

In business, we must be on the lookout for performance and growth killers at all times. That's one of the key reasons for the 12 Warning Signs of Success—to help you focus on simplicity and fight against complexity.

Now let's see what it looks like to actually do this.

SEVEN

LEADERSHIP

THE FIRST FIVE WARNING SIGNS OF SUCCESS

DON'T BE AFRAID TO FIRST LOOK IN THE MIRROR FOR WARNING signs of success. Are *you* the problem? Is your leadership team making matters worse or improving the situation? Remember what I said at the beginning of the book. You have to be honest about the situation. You may be able to fool everyone else, but do not fool yourself!

No amount of sales, marketing, neatly crafted core values or previous success can overcome incompetent leadership.

You'll never know if you don't examine the first few warning signs of success to determine what, if anything, needs attention on your journey through the Business Growth Cycle.

THE FIRST WARNING SIGN OF SUCCESS: **RIGHT IDEA, WRONG PERSON**

KNOW THIS: Getting and keeping the *right people at the right time* on the team is critical to a leader's success. If you get the right team in place, the rest of the work is infinitely easier. But everyone who has ever hired or promoted anyone has screwed it up at least once.

FEEL THIS: Hiring, promoting and firing naturally feel personal—because we're all human. Pay careful attention to your gut. Do not tell yourself the sweet little lie that you are not good at hiring or are not good at having difficult conversations with underperformers. Follow the truth outlined in this warning sign.

DO THIS: Take an honest look at your situation. If the team member causing you angst interviewed for this position today, would you hire that person again? Ask this about every person on your team. This is your business; you can't afford anything but the best. Every dollar you're paying the wrong employee is a missed opportunity to hire a rock star! Have tough conversations—both with yourself and with the problem employee. Be brave enough to tell the truth and move forward with purpose.

The need to hire someone is a sign of success; you cannot do all of it yourself anymore. It's time to grow—that's the goal of all businesses.

The dirty little secret about this area of growth is that everyone who has hired or promoted anyone—regardless of the size of the business or years of experience—has made at least one hiring or promoting mistake. There's no doubt you will too. It's impossible to get this right every time.

What you *can* get better at is determining the criteria for these decisions, assessing shortly down the line whether you have the wrong person and shortening your time spent tolerating that person.

I once heard Peter Drucker say something to the effect, "No one would argue it takes the right person to get the job done, yet when we are hiring or promoting someone we get it right about

Right Idea, Wrong Person Matrix

Let's face it, teams have winners, under-performers and destructive performers. Who on your team knows how to win, and who needs to be asked to leave?

Charting Your Team Dynamic

Map the coordinates on the Dando Team Assessment Matrix by rating your team members from 0 to10 in the categories of Attitude and overall Performance.

1) Start with the vertical side of the chart labeled Attitude. Move your finger up the left side of the chart and stop on the number that you feel fits your team member's attitude toward the business and their work: personality, works well with others, cultural fit, etc. (Please note: 0 is the lowest and 10 is the highest.)

2) Now rate your team member from 0 to 10 on the horizontal Performance side of the grid. Move your finger across the horizontal side of the chart and stop on the number you feel fits your team member's level of performance in terms of ability to get desired results and help the business win. (Please note: 0 is the lowest and 10 is the highest.)

3) Map the coordinates by connecting the placement of the vertical and horizontal lines. Do this for each team member to see how the whole team maps out.

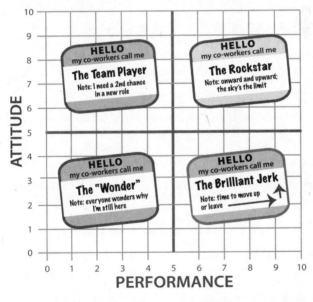

This team member has a positive, infectious attitude, but needs your leadership to continue to evolve. The business may have outgrown their ability to perform in their current role, and they may need your coaching to reach, or get back to Rockstar status.

The Team Player — Note: need a 2nd chance in a new role

This is your go-to team member. They quietly, but effectively, make the business and everyone around them better. Load your team with these winners.

The Rockstar — Note: onward and upward; the sky's the limit

Everyone, even you, wonders how this person got on the team. Don't look the other way and allow a weak link to bring down the entire team. Take immediate action, because choosing to keep this person on board is a losing proposition.

The "Wonder" — Note: everyone wonders why I'm still here

These team members may make the business a lot of money and/or perform well in their roles but they can destroy a team. **Don't be held hostage by these Brilliant Jerks.** They are holding your business back. If you're going to grow, you have to help them figure out how to become a Rockstar, or get rid of them.

The Brilliant Jerk — Note: time to move up or leave

Figure 14

⅓ of the time, ⅓ of the time it is average and ⅓ of the time it is terrible . . . there is no other area of business where we would tolerate such poor performance as we do in the hiring and promoting of people."

My Right Idea, Wrong Person matrix (figure 14) helps you determine where a team member falls on the scale and what the next steps can be.

A very successful CEO I work with wasn't sure that a low-performing team member's work habits were egregious enough to warrant termination. Here are the three questions I asked him that helped him decide what to do. Think about these if you're struggling with a potentially "wrong person."

1. What's your instinct? On a scale of 0 to 10 (0 being terrible, 10 being fantastic), how would you rate this team member's attitude or cultural fit in the company? (The CEO answered, "About a 5.")
2. On the same scale of 0 to 10, how would you rate this team member's performance? (The CEO answered, "About a 7.")
3. If this team member interviewed for this position today, and you knew what you know now about this team member, would you hire this person? (The CEO's answer was a quick "*No!*")

He had his answer. Here's what's enlightening about this example:

- I always ask leaders to share their instincts, because personnel issues are very often vague, debatable, and gut wrenching! If you feel you cannot trust your instincts—which should naturally incorporate your past experiences—it's worth taking a time-out to explore why.

Learning to trust yourself is like building muscle: It is not easy and it takes time, but the resulting strength is well worth it.

- I pointed out the subtle but critical fact that he had rejected interviewees who had given far fewer warning signs than this current team member gave him. Though his company, like most, had a great process to pressure-test people during the interviewing process, once someone makes it onto the team, the leadership team unknowingly goes soft on their expectations. In effect, they never pressure-test a team member's ability to win on an ongoing basis—for the long haul. We all have seen an interviewee shine, then send their evil twin to work. We're left wondering what happened and hoping the person we interviewed someday comes back. Ongoing accountability and consistently high expectations are critical. Hiring key team members is never a "set it and forget it" proposition. Just like you, as a leader, don't rest on your laurels, neither should anyone else.

- By asking the three questions listed above and using the Right Idea, Wrong Person matrix, you can continue to make sure the people on your team are clear about your expectations and what *winning* looks like.

Your rock star team members expect a lot from themselves, and they expect managers to hold high standards for all team members. If you don't maintain a high level of discipline for your *current team members and interviewees,* you're running the risk that the mediocre people will chase away those rock stars. We all know that problem employees require more attention and work than the ones who are crushing it. So while it may feel totally counterintuitive, for the next 30 days, spend most of your time with your top performers, not your underperformers. The results will be powerful. Remember: You get what you set yourself up for.

In another situation, I worked with a company that planned to go public within the next two years, and the finance team was busily preparing. The new CFO had experience taking companies public and was respected by the executive team and the board, but there was trouble brewing. He consistently got negative feedback from his employees in quarterly management feedback cycles.

By the next cycle, there was a bigger problem: Not a single member on the team gave any feedback on him.

The silence was deafening.

The CEO, concerned about the culture and the team's future performance, called a meeting with everyone except the CFO. He learned the team was miserable; they felt demoralized, abused, unheard.

According to my Right Idea, Wrong Person matrix, the CEO was dealing with what is known as a brilliant jerk. In the company's entire history, nobody had ever made such a universally negative impression as this man had. The CEO had big plans for the company—going public required a strong, experienced CFO. But it was equally important that that person fit in the culture of openness, teamwork and respect.

The CEO and leadership team acted quickly. The CFO was let go, and the CEO brought all the employees together to explain that the CFO was not a culture fit, that the CEO would not tolerate brilliant jerks and while it would be tough to operate without a CFO for the coming weeks or months, it was the right decision. His actions were transparent to the entire team, making it clear that if similar situations occurred, he wanted to know about them so he could deal with them. It was scary but motivating for the whole company—far beyond just the finance team—and a key indicator of the CEO's commitment to putting the right people in place.

Building on what they had learned, the CEO, the leadership team and the finance team worked together to find the right CFO, one with both experience and real respect for the company culture.

Warning Signs: How Do You Know If You're Working with the Wrong Person?

Pay attention—really pay attention—to these warning signs. Do you see your situation here anywhere?

- You get a sick feeling in your stomach every time you have to deal with this person.
- Knowing what you know now, if this person interviewed for their position again, your reaction would be an automatic "No!"
- This person is not a rock star—or even heading in that direction—in the Right Idea, Wrong Person matrix.
- This person makes a lot of excuses and shows little forward movement.
- You get negative feedback on this person from multiple sources, and similar feedback from several areas of the organization. Every time you get feedback, ask for the root cause. Is it a personality issue, skills or competency, misaligned expectations? All of these require different follow-up actions.
- This person consistently misses goals.
- You find yourself doing this person's job.
- There is frequent turnover in a key role or team directly related or adjacent to this person.

Root Cause: Here's the *Real* Problem

So why is this happening? When you get to the root cause—the "why"—you can take effective action. But this will require focused thinking and honest conversations. Here are some potential root causes for this situation:

- You have a weak or outdated hiring and promoting process.
- The current job description doesn't distinguish the must-haves from the nice-to-haves, or delineate the nonnegotiable personal characteristics. In short, the true job description—as it stands today, not as it was when the person joined the team—doesn't match the person's skills or personality.
- The person you hired doesn't truly have the skills needed to succeed.
- The position's goals and metrics are not clear.
- The role has evolved beyond the individual's capabilities.
- You wrote the job description with this person already in mind instead of writing the job description for what you really need.
- There are few or no quality standards for the review process. The reviewer doesn't have clear instructions about what to uncover, results are inconclusive, reviews are based on the personal needs or tastes of the reviewer, or the review never happens. Reviews must combine measurable metrics and insights into soft skills—how the individual interacts with team members, for example—and they should be balanced, based on the type of position the reviewee holds.

Problem Solving: Triage Your Current Situation

Soon you'll get out of problem-solving mode because you'll build your problem-predicting muscles—and you won't find yourself in this situation again. For now, though, you need quick, immediately effective solutions. Remember: We get what we set ourselves up for. Take a moment to honestly assess where you are right now, so you can move ahead with purpose.

- Determine the real root cause or causes, not just the symptoms, from the list in the previous section. Getting clarity here helps you solve the problem. Here are some keys to determining the root cause:
  - Where does the person fall in the Right Idea, Wrong Person matrix?
  - Do you have the right idea—the right job description, the correct understanding of what the role truly is? Or do you have the wrong idea for the actual role? Have you changed your expectations for the role?
  - If you determine that you have the right idea but the results are not what you expected or wanted, look again at the person. Do you have the wrong person?
  - If you have the wrong idea, is that why you have the wrong person? What needs to change—the idea or the person?
- If you can identify the root cause—and it's not the wrong person—great! Read on to discover the problem-predicting strategies so you can keep moving. Take steps to improve your hiring and recruiting process or review process.
- If you do, in fact, have the wrong person, take action promptly. Nobody likes transitioning an employee out of the business. It's gut wrenching and anxiety inducing and feels very personal. That's why admitting that you have a wrong person is so hard! But sooner is *always* better here: If you hesitate, you're setting yourself up for a much bigger train wreck. The truth is, by the time you realize you have the wrong person, it's probably unbearable for the people working alongside him or her. And please, don't begin

transitioning the person but leave him or her in place for a short time as a courtesy. Rip off that bandage; you can give the person a severance package to help yourself feel better, if you like, but get that person's team members out of their misery as quickly as possible.

Problem Predicting: Build These Muscles to Avoid This Tough Situation in the Future

The real growth comes from surviving these situations, then building processes and systems that prevent the problem from happening again. *If you take your team out of problem-solving mode, they'll use their brain cells to innovate and move the business forward—where you want it to go.*

To reduce the odds of hiring or promoting the wrong person again, create a hiring process that tests for skills and culture fit and that sets expectations before you even write the job description. It's time to go back to the very beginning and make sure every part of the process focuses on your company's key goals.

Here are three key steps I recommend to build a great hiring process. I know the temptation to water this down is very strong, but don't! Follow through, because there's nothing more important than getting the *right* people into your business.

- *Go beyond the traditional job description.* Sometimes the wrong person is the result of a lack of alignment about the purpose of the role. If you never really agree on the right idea, you'll never have the right person. Huddle up with the key stakeholders and discuss not only the job description, but all of the following as well:
  - What are the must-haves versus the nice-to-haves?
  - What are the nonnegotiable personal characteristics and behaviors required for this role?

 • If this person is wildly successful, what specific measurable and nonmeasurable results will we see one year from now?
 • What would the right person in this role accomplish in the first 90 days?
 • *How* do you expect this person to achieve these results? For example, will the person work with an existing team, command and control or collaborate across the business?

- *Look for the right candidates.* Source candidates directly within the industry or related industries. Reach out to your business network and place appropriate advertising. And recruit beyond your own network. It's easy to hire people who are known, but you or your colleagues may not already know the best person for the job. Be patient but very persistent . . . it is worth it!

- *Try dating before marrying.* Once you have narrowed the selection of candidates to two or three, ask each of them to prepare a plan of what they would do in the first 90 days, which they will present to key stakeholders. Or have each candidate do a bit of role-playing. For example, if the candidate is going to be in a sales position, have your team play the clients and ask the candidate to give a full sales pitch for your product. Or, if the candidate will be in a technical role, give him an existing software problem and have him present a solution. Get creative and have some fun, but do not skip this important step.

- *Don't be overly prescriptive about what you're looking for.* Give your candidates some flexibility to demonstrate their own resourcefulness, creativity and ability to think independently. This will speak volumes about how they will perform if you decide to hire them. And don't give them more than two or three days to prepare a presentation. On the job, sometimes all we have is a weekend or overnight to prepare for a meeting with a major customer, our team or the board of directors.

- *Give your candidates the contact information for key people* who can answer any questions they have during the process. After the presentation, find out if they talked to any of these people. Could their presentation have been better with more information? Did they use their resources?

- When you invite key stakeholders to the candidate's presentation, *make sure they have copies of the job description,* including the must-haves versus the nice-to-haves. Have an honest conversation with stakeholders right after the presentation to make a decision based on facts and instincts.

- *Make sure each candidate knows he or she will have 45 minutes to present,* no more. Encourage them to leave time for questions in that 45 minutes. After the presentation, dismiss the candidate and have your team spend 15 minutes discussing the candidate and making a decision. If you allow people to start asking too many questions of the candidate, you risk your team trying to lead a candidate to give the answers you're looking for. Remember: You want your team to look forward to these presentations, and if they drag on or if the process becomes painful, the value will break down. Keep them to 45 minutes and 15 minutes for Q&A!

One last tip: Remove time from the equation. Too often in hiring, we're reacting to the seemingly insurmountable pile of work that must get done *right now.* It's very difficult to look beyond this short-term crisis and take the time to make the *right* decision, not just the easiest, *fastest* decision. Remember, you hired the wrong person before, and it turned out to be far more trouble than any temporary work crunch. Don't make the same mistake twice.

This sounds daunting, but, like everything else, good planning makes everything else a piece of cake.

So What? Now What?

Hiring, firing, promoting and transitioning team members are some of the most challenging responsibilities you'll face as a leader—and you'll never get them exactly right every time. But avoiding the Right Idea, Wrong Person challenge from the beginning greatly helps you streamline hiring and be *completely honest* about who has the right skills and is the best fit.

THE SECOND WARNING SIGN OF SUCCESS:
BAD MANAGEMENT OF GREAT OPPORTUNITIES

KNOW THIS: Moving from *doing* to *managing* is one of the toughest transitions in anyone's career. You must know the subtle but significant differences that separate a technical genius, a managerial leader and a leader. Not only must you know how and when to apply these skill sets in order to grow; you have to be able to predict the need for these skills—before they're needed. The future growth and sustainability of your organization *depend* on your getting this right.

FEEL THIS: You are not alone! Every leader has dealt with this warning sign of success and likely learned this lesson the hard way. When you break tradition by *not* making this mistake, your organization can soar. You appreciate and even love the people who helped you start this venture. You want them to grow with the business, and when they don't, it really hurts. Their lack of ability to make the seemingly easy transition from doing to managing can feel like a betrayal to you: Don't they care enough to do this right? But if you fire them, they'll feel betrayed by you. It feels personal. As leaders we often tell ourselves the sweet little lies that cause us to *give in* to what we see as chaos—believing it's impossible to find the right people, we are being too picky, and so on—and then we *give up*. We *give up* the hope of harnessing the chaos. I am here to tell you the chaos can be harnessed.

DO THIS: Set your organization up for success early and often by thinking ahead to the management skills you'll need. It's undeniable: You'll definitely need managerial talent as you grow. Think about how to introduce this conversation into your team's discussion about growth. Do not make it personal; make it about winning. Honest conversation is one of the best gifts we can give; get honest with yourself and your leadership team. Take personality and likability out of the equation; get clear about the exact skills you need, before you need them, for each technical genius, managerial leader and leadership role; then see where the specific gaps are. Once your leadership team—the right leadership team—starts to flesh this out, the process becomes empowering. You'll begin to see the sky's the limit for your business.

As a business grows, it's usually not the *lack* of great opportunities that causes growth to halt. It's the *bad management* of great opportunities that trips you up.

When you started out, it was all hands on deck. Every person on the team created value, and quickly. You couldn't have gotten going—all the way up to the Level 2 company that you likely are today—without them. They created the product, the market and everything else from the ground up.

As the company grew, there was plenty to do. You promoted these early team members; many now have leadership roles. But growth and progress have stalled. You're fighting the same battles again and again. Your staff is still growing, but the work isn't going any faster; you're not getting where you thought you would. You're beginning to wonder what happened to your Start-up Wonder Team.

Fact is, you needed the technical geniuses, the ones with raw skill and experience, who could execute quickly to get your business started. They're so good at what they do that they can do it with their eyes closed. I call these folks "unconsciously competent." But here's the dirty little secret: Most people don't have the skills, experience and inherent talent to be a good managerial leader, much less a visionary leader. In general, 90% of team members are great technical geniuses; they do their core skill and operate in their comfort zone very well. But only 9% have the natural talent to be good managerial leaders, and only 1% of all people have the raw talent to be true leaders.

In short, any time you promote someone to a managerial role, you have a less than 10% chance of getting it right. I am not saying that you are either born a leader or not. I am saying, for most of us, it takes a tremendous amount of growth, persistence and hard work to make the transition from doing to leading.

You've taken someone who is so good that he is unconsciously competent at his technical skill. You've put him in a managerial leader role—you both feel he earned it. He feels good about it—especially the pay increase—but now he is "unconsciously incompetent": he doesn't know what he doesn't know when it comes to managing and leading.

So off he goes to a 12-week leadership development course. Or you give him ten management books to read. This is the equivalent of putting lipstick on a pig. There is an entire industry that takes advantage of the false hope that great doers can become passionate and skilled managers and leaders with just a few easy bullet points. Chances are, there's an in-law or spouse telling them how much more money they can make as managers or leaders, so they're all in for moving on up. This is not wrong, it is just often underestimated how hard it is to make this transition . . . you have to really, really want it!

Great technical geniuses have strong personal responsibility, know their jobs very well, and see how their jobs fit into the bigger team and organization. It may have taken years to get to this point of being so skilled, or it could be a natural talent combined with training. These people are *absolutely critical* to the success of every organization and are the ones who really know how to get things done.

But a management role takes a whole different set of skills. Think about it: What are some of the characteristics of the best managers or leaders you have ever worked for? They may be learned, but many are not. You probably think of a good manager as someone who acts as a conduit between the people and the overall goals of the organization, deploying the resources available to get the desired outcomes. They are great delegators, yet they never dump jobs they just don't want to do on everyone else. They are coaches and teachers; they feel a strong sense of responsibility for others; they are great listeners and advisors—the list goes on.

Given all that, it's not surprising that only about 10% of team members have these inherent gifts or are interested in leaving their comfort zone to get, practice and perfect these needed skills.

Of course, management training and good books can help. But it also takes experience, training, good instincts and an unusual level of commitment that goes beyond the pay and benefits. You truly have to get what I call a "helper's high" to want to become a great manager or leader.

Even rarer are the 1% of people who have the raw talent to be transformational leaders. They're visionary, empowering to others, inherently growth oriented and never satisfied with the status quo—measured risk takers who trust their intuition, which rarely lets them down.

Are managers and leaders born or made? Debates rage about this, and the truth is, there may be some natural-born leaders, but for most people—90% of people—managing or leading is really, really hard work. Most people don't do this work—they take a 12-week leadership training course, negotiate a leadership title or get promoted because of the sheer laziness or ineptitude of a previous manager.

The finer points of great management or leadership have filled many other books. What you must understand is that great managers and leaders must have a *burning desire* to get out of their comfort zone and develop others—and probably give them most of the credit for anything that gets done.

As Jeremie Kubicek points out in his book *Leadership Is Dead: How Influence Is Reviving It,* the most important question you will never be asked as a leader is, "Are you for me, against me or for yourself?" Think about your former bosses: How would you answer this question about them? More important, how would your team answer this question about *you?*

Figure 15

TEAM MEMBER CHARACTERISTICS

Technical Genius	Managerial Leader	Leader
• Performs individually • Learns one or a few skills well • Identifies with the workers • Has a strong responsibility for self • Sees big picture of own job • Communicates clearly • Takes responsibility for skills • Operates best in technical comfort zone	• Is an effective delegator • Is a coach/teacher • Can deal with conflict • Identifies with management • Is deadline oriented • Is operations oriented • Is detail oriented • Is methodical • Has strong responsibility for others • Sees big picture of all jobs • Assembles productive teams • Is worth following	• Is a visionary • Has a high level of commitment • Empowers others • Is inspirational • Is perceived as a risk taker • Knows personal limitations • Achieves balance through others • Sees big picture of company • Trusts intuitive direction • Is growth oriented

Adapted from Bob Beale of Beale International. Reprinted with permission.

Warning Signs: How Do You Know If You're Mired in Bad Management of a Great Opportunity?

You may notice that some of the warning signs are the same as those in Right Idea, Wrong Person. Because both Warning Signs of Success deal with people, there is meaningful overlap—but do not let this confuse you. Right Idea, Wrong Person can happen anywhere and at any level in your organization. Bad Management of a Great Opportunity deals specifically with managers in your organization. Going from "doing" to "managing" is the toughest transition in anyone's career; if you cannot learn to identify the difference between a technician, manager and leader and get each of them properly placed in your organization you will significantly impair your ability to grow . . . or worse. Dig deep here to see which Warning Sign of Success you are dealing with. So pay attention—really pay attention—to these warning signs. Do you see your situation here anywhere?

- Seemingly great growth opportunities consistently escape your grasp.
- There is frequent turnover in a certain team or teams.
- Metrics goals are consistently missed, even though the forecasts were agreed to and thought to be reasonable.
- A manager is hiring or promoting people that are not as good or smart as that manager. (A sure sign of a poor manager is his reluctance to hire someone smarter than he is.)
- A manager consistently complains that "if it is going to get done right, I have to do it myself." That manager may have a lousy team in place, or he doesn't know how to delegate; either case is a signal of a bad manager.
- Knowing what you know now, if this person interviewed for the same position again, your reaction would be an automatic "No!"
- This person may be a rock star in the Right Idea, Wrong Person matrix for his *technical* role, but evaluated on his *management* role, this person is not a rock star. Determining the difference in the roles requires thought, so take the time to understand the difference between the technician and manager roles using the "Team Member Characteristics" chart.
- You get negative feedback from people who work for and with this manager. Every time you get feedback, ask for the root cause. Is it a personality issue, skills or competency, or misaligned expectations?

- This person's team seems generally confused about what's expected of them, and the manager has plenty of excuses whenever he misses key goals.
- You find yourself doing this manager's job.
- You get a sick feeling in your stomach every time you have to deal with this person.

Root Cause: Here's the *Real* Problem

So why is this happening? You can't move forward until you truly understand the root cause.

- The person in the role doesn't truly have the skills needed to succeed.
- The role has evolved beyond the individual's skills or capabilities. (Or the individual never had the management skills needed for this role to begin with.)
- You have a weak, outdated or nonexistent process for promoting team members.
- The current job description—if you even have one—doesn't delineate the must-haves from the nice-to-haves or define the nonnegotiable personal characteristics for the role. In short, the true job description doesn't match the person.
- You wrote the job description with this person already in mind instead of writing the job description for what you really need. This is a huge mistake that's often made, especially during the time between Level 1/Start-up and Level 2/Hyper-Growth, when you feel you "owe" someone a promotion for sweating through Level 1 with you. Always—always!—resist putting names into an organizational chart before you accurately and completely define the roles. Then make sure you're matching the skills

and experience of the person with the specific needs of that role. It must be a near-perfect match, no exceptions.

- Goals and metrics are not clear.

Problem Solving: Triage Your Current Situation

Soon you'll get out of problem-solving mode because you'll build your problem-predicting muscles—and you won't find yourself in this situation again. For now, though, you need quick solutions to get you out of this immediate situation.

- Write a job description for the *position*—not for the *person* who currently holds the position. What would you see in 90 days if the person in this role were successful? What are the nonnegotiables, the ideal experience level, the skills you really need for this position, if you were hiring for it for the first time? This can be tough, because you're thinking about the person who is causing you angst, but it's very important. Enlist the help of someone who's experienced with this type of position and not directly involved in this situation for a fresh, honest perspective.
- Have you already given this person every opportunity to gain the needed skills? Does this person show the commitment to work hard to get the skills needed? Is there a course this employee could take, a mentor he or she could shadow? If so, provide these opportunities and instill a sense of urgency.
- Using the list from the Root Cause section above, get very, very clear on the root cause.
  - Where does the person fall in the Right Idea, Wrong Person matrix? Is there a real chance this person could make it as a manager?

- What specific skills is this person lacking? Are they trainable skills, or does the job take instincts that are simply not there and that won't be there anytime soon?

- If you determine that there's no saving this person in his or her current role, take action promptly. Nobody ever wants to have to transition someone out of the business; it's gut wrenching and feels very personal—after all, this person may have been with you since the beginning. But sooner rather than later is the key here. Fact is, once you know you have a problem, it's likely much worse than you think for the people working alongside this person.

Problem Predicting: Build These Muscles to Avoid This Tough Situation in the Future

Here is how this situation could have been avoided with some advance planning—way back when you are a Level 1 business.

Here's what happens: We start a business with a core group of people, or we hire some people early on. A few months or a year into it, we start planning for the future: It's exciting to look at the organization chart as it grows into the company of our dreams. Look at all the opportunity—especially leadership roles!—we'll create for people.

Then it happens. We look around the table and we put names in those boxes on the organization chart. Or the accounting guru assumes he'll be CFO today, despite the fact that he was hired as an intern last year. Or the coder with six years of experience believes he'll be CTO in 18 months. They think, either consciously or unconsciously, "I'm here at the beginning. I'm owed that job." In any case, once a name is in the box—physically or mentally—it feels like a done deal.

But this is where you can literally change the future of your organization—turning it from an "accidental" success (which it may seem like it is today, because you feel you got some lucky breaks) into an intentional powerhouse.

Here's how: *You don't put names in those boxes.* Instead, you get very clear about the skills, experience and nonnegotiable traits that will make each role extremely successful. You have got to align the purpose and goals of your organization with the resources you *will need,* not necessarily the resources you *currently have.* As a team, you look beyond the talent that's in the room and focus on the very specific goals you set earlier in the strategic planning meeting.

This will feel awkward. You consider many of the people around you friends. If nothing else, you need them right now to keep the company growing like crazy, so you want to motivate them by showing them what is possible for them. But you can't afford to be short-sighted; you must think about the future of the organization beyond this team—*even beyond yourself.* You and your team must define what is needed, and it is up to the individuals to make it possible but *not* to assume or feel entitled. Any promotions must be clearly earned based on the objective needs—not based on emotions, a sense of owing someone a job or any other reason! Focus on the facts.

By creating the list of core skills required for each of these aspirational roles, you're creating a clear road map for your company. If the intern really wants to become CFO, he'll know precisely how to get there—and you can give him access to training and mentors to help him gain the skills he doesn't yet have. There will be no illusions.

This sounds daunting, but, like everything else, well-thought-out planning (problem predicting) makes everything else a piece of cake.

Here's how to build this process:

- Look at the business's overall goals, then tap into exactly how this role—not the person, but the role—precisely fits into these goals. The metrics for success should become crystal clear.
- Involve the team in writing job descriptions for key roles.
- Create a list of the specific business skills and experience it takes to effectively meet the desired metrics. For example, if the business goal is to lead a sales team that grows sales 120% over the next five years, you want to find someone who has already achieved this in a similarly sized company.
- Beyond specific skills, what are the nonnegotiables everyone on your team needs? The ability to collaborate, flexibility, nimbleness, a passion for your company's cause? Think about your company's culture. What are the things about your company you want people to know from the beginning and be excited about?
- Write job descriptions honestly and specifically, and be accurate about what you state as must-haves (nonnegotiable for success) and nice-to-haves (specific experience doing this exact job in your same industry).
- Think beyond the start-up phase you're in now. A "go-go-go!" mentality may be what keeps things moving today, but the future may demand a different posture. What are the skills and experience your organization will value when you're a Level 3 organization?

So What? Now What?

Hiring, firing, promoting and transitioning team members are some of the most challenging responsibilities you'll face as a leader—and you'll never get them just right every time. Avoiding the challenge from the beginning helps you streamline hiring and be completely honest about who has the right skills and is the best fit. It also helps your team members know exactly what it takes to grow into their aspirational roles—you may not hire a CTO for several years, so maybe your start-up guy can add to his skill set to serve you well there.

Once you get clear on what you need in a role, don't equivocate. Some people may feel discouraged by the org chart, may even get angry, feeling they're entitled to high-ranking, high-paid roles. Others will see it as an exciting challenge and rise to the occasion. Still others will see clearly that, for now, they're in the right role for this time in the company's history and may be great second lieutenants a few years down the road.

I cannot overstate the importance of this forward thinking. I promise you, figuring this out *before* you get in the gut-wrenching position of facing a crisis and having to get rid of a good technician who may have never had what it took to be a great manager will be a great service to them, you and your team in the long run.

THE THIRD WARNING SIGN OF SUCCESS: **OPEN DOOR, CLOSED MIND**

KNOW THIS: Even the best teams—ones that eventually unlock real success—suffer through crises that leave them feeling out of control, disjointed and exhausted. Change is inevitable, but growth is a choice. Most often, growth is limited and the best team members leave because someone in a leadership position has stopped growing; she is operating from her comfort zone. This way of operating served her and the business at a smaller size and earlier time, but now she cannot hear good ideas, see warning signs or lead beyond where she has been.

FEEL THIS: You and/or someone on your team feels like the business has grown to a size and complexity this leader has never been responsible for. Watch out for this sweet little lie we start to tell ourselves. You or your team members are overwhelmed, are not sure where to start and react defensively to new ideas and people. It feels like you're in a rocket ship speeding toward a wall called "I do not know what I do not know." Team members feel like they have the responsibility but do not have the authority or at least some latitude in how they approach getting the desired results.

DO THIS: Acknowledge this feeling and have an open, honest conversation with the team, without blame. It's time to restate the team's specific goals and get to the heart of why you're not achieving them. Trust the people you have hired to get the job done and hold them accountable for results. And start with yourself; what fears or challenges are you facing? How can you do the job differently or better? Being open to feedback yourself can make others more open to feedback. Chances are, a "we're all on the same team" talk can drive real solutions, but you must respectfully and honestly air the specific problems plaguing the team.

When a mind is closed, even the clearest presentation of the facts will not open it!

You and your leadership team say you're on board for change and growth, but your actions tell a different story. You dismiss ideas quickly, impede others from introducing new processes, micromanage or control details rather than trust people to do their jobs or shut down completely whenever there's conflict.

Negativity or insecurity seep into the team, and people start to play it safe—working "not to lose" rather than working to win. Things spiral down from there. As situations become more uncertain or fear prevails, people go into "control" mode, thinking, "If it's going to get done, I'll have to do it myself." They stop working as a team, stop leading.

It's time to unlock, uncover and find real leadership.

I worked with a company that started a new division within their organization, and the team was really scrappy—they had a directive to move fast, they set aggressive goals and the product they created was great. But after three months, they couldn't show sales metrics, so the team leader feared that it meant they hadn't actually accomplished anything.

This couldn't be further from the truth: The team had created sound marketing and sales processes, had clear messaging and was getting buy-in from all the right people. They were well on their way to executing a marketing plan to gain 600 leads. But all the team leader talked about was closed deals. He relentlessly grilled the team: "Where are the deals? Why are we one-third of the way into the quarter but we've only closed 10% of our quota?" Out of fear and poor communication, he went into "control" mode and started giving directives: "Fire our agency! Everybody—even the engineers and marketers—must make ten sales calls in the next hour! Obviously the marketing plan is crap; I'll rethink it! Don't think, don't question, just go!" It was a classic case of thinking that looking busy or working long hours meant that the right things were happening.

The team was exhausted and frustrated. The lack of focus on—or even honest conversation about—the true, core problems (trading business for measurable results) meant no decisions could be made; ambiguity abounded. The right hand didn't know what the left hand was doing. Instead of thinking strategically or staying the course, the team was constantly reacting to the leader's (often contradictory) demands. So the real work couldn't move forward. Worse, the team spent a lot of time grumbling about how the leader was a control freak. One by one, team members quit the team or quit the company. It was months before the poor manager—who had been promoted to his current position because he'd been at the company forever—was finally removed from the company, and by that time all momentum had completely stalled. Fact was, the project looked like such a mess from the outside that nobody wanted to take it on.

Open Door, Closed Mind is a surefire way to run off your most talented team members. These were the ones who admired your past success and wanted to join in for the ride, but now they're saddled with managers who *say* they trust the team and want new ideas, but their actions tell a completely different story. This particular poor manager had actively poached the best and brightest from the rest of the company, then never let them work to their full potential.

Open Door, Closed Mind is also a surefire indication that you don't have clarity around the four or five measurable goals of your business. I cannot overstate this: Once your goals are clear, it's actually simple—not *easy,* but *simple*—to know precisely where to focus.

Warning Signs: How Do You Know If You or Your Team Is Mired in an "Open Door, Closed Mind" Mentality?

As with every one of these warning signs, it all begins with being truly honest with yourself. Take some time to really reflect on what is going wrong, why you're allowing fear to drive your actions. And bring your team together to speak honestly.

Pay attention—really pay attention—to these warning signs. Do you see your situation here anywhere?

- Your team tells you that they see a disconnect between the company's official policy of "bring us your ideas" and the way their managers actually react to team member suggestions. You see a lot of activity—the team is exhausted and busy—but you can't see the results.
- You feel paralyzed; you're not sure what to do next. You wonder if your passion for the business will ever return.
- You have meetings upon meetings that don't lead anywhere.

- You're not getting good ideas from your team anymore, just half-baked ideas that sound suspiciously like what they might think you want to hear.
- Customer feedback indicates that they feel undervalued and/or not heard.
- You still hold regular brainstorming sessions, but the resulting ideas are never implemented. The idea machine simply pumps out unicorns and fairy dust.

Root Cause: Here's the *Real* Problem

So why is this happening? You can't move forward until you truly understand the root cause.

- You either don't have clear goals or you don't know how to effectively measure and create positive accountability around them. Without this true north, you cannot determine *what* to do or—more important—what *not* to do. This sounds like a subtle difference, but it's not. We've all spent time doing projects that took forever and ended up netting nothing. I knew a company that was so focused on building a fun "culture"—with plenty of T-shirts, parties and free food for the team—that just two weeks after their huge annual party, they laid off 20% of the workforce. Why do we get distracted by doing the wrong things? Because we think that activity—any activity—is more fruitful than taking time to reflect and really plan what should be done next. As you know by now, this is 100% wrong.
- It's you. You're stuck in "fear" mode, you're insecure and it's paralyzing you. The lies you told yourself have kept you from facing the issues head-on, and now they are making you paranoid. For whatever reason, either you have stopped

growing and stretching yourself or you do not trust the people on your team to get the results you and they have agreed to. Remember, I said you must be completely honest with yourself. It's much easier to put the blame elsewhere. Who wants to admit that they're a problem, much less do the arduous work of remedying the problem? What if you discover that you shouldn't be leading the company at all, that the entire team is miserable because of you? Where does that leave you? I get it. It feels terrifying. But you must get to ground truth before anything can move forward. If you really shouldn't be in charge, chances are you're miserable anyway; maybe it's time to give the reins to someone else, step aside and let the business be successful, and do something you find enjoyable. You have to be open to scrutinizing your best friends or family members in this process; it applies to you, too. You owe it to the business and to those who have invested in you, and maybe you owe it to yourself and your family most of all!

- You manage the process, but not the pace or the results. You reward people for working hard—putting in long hours, making personal sacrifices and creating reams of reports and analyses. But none of it is tied to results.

Problem Solving: Triage Your Current Situation

Soon you'll get out of problem-solving mode because you'll build your problem-predicting muscles—and you won't find yourself in this situation again. For now, though, you need quick solutions to get you out of this immediate situation.

- If you think the problem is you, sit your team down and apologize to them. If you ask your team if they think you're stuck in Open Door, Closed Mind and they hesitate or don't answer, take that as a yes. Let them know that you never intended to close your mind, and show your humanity by sharing your reasons—if you can pinpoint them.

- Collaborate with your team about how to solve the current problem and how to move forward. Asking for their help is the very first step in training yourself out of Open Door, Closed Mind.

- Reevaluate your goals, metrics and instrumentation to track success, so you make informed decisions. What motivates people is a sense of accomplishment. As Zig Ziglar said, "Aiming at nothing will guarantee the direct hit."[1]

All these actions hinge on having open, authentic relationships among the leadership team. People simply must be able to speak honestly. True leaders are brave enough to do this, and the best communicators can share negative feedback without being harsh. Chances are, you or your team is in this very situation because you *don't* encourage open conversation. So it's long past time to change that, and it should begin with you. Be humble, human and brave enough to get to the truth; it's the only way you'll get to a solution.

Problem Predicting: Build These Muscles to Avoid This Tough Situation in the Future

The real growth comes from surviving these situations, and then—instead of putting your head down until the next crisis—building processes and systems that prevent the problem from happening again.

- Think and talk about how this situation came about. Was fear taking over? Were we distracted by the Next Big Thing? Did a competitor throw us off track?

- Hire a team of badasses and get out of the way. Hire
  people better than you. (By the way, most people who are
  in a position of leadership cannot do this. Real leaders,
  however, do it again and again. Most effective leaders
  surround themselves with the best.)
- Start using the term "Open Door, Closed Mind" in
  leadership and board meetings, and share how you
  persevered through it. This can happen to any team—and
  it will topple the very best of us. Keeping this top of mind
  is the first step in ensuring it doesn't happen again.

So What? Now What?

Open Door, Closed Mind can manifest itself in many ways, but
it will always sap your team of their mojo, stunt growth, derail
progress and topple your team faster than you can imagine.

The two principles to keep in mind in this situation are, "Am I
letting fear take over here? Have I stopped growing myself?" and
"Are we worrying about the right things?" Fear and confusion
create a powerful and vicious cycle.

THE FOURTH WARNING SIGN OF SUCCESS:
THE LEADERSHIP BOTTLENECK

KNOW THIS: Organizational structure drives behavior. It is impossible to have
the structure of a jellyfish and behave like a cheetah. As an organization
grows, you must have radically different leadership practices. No firm ever
draws an organizational structure so it looks like a rake—that is, there's one
person at the top and everyone else reports to that person, either by straight
line or dotted line—but if you play back the tape, that is exactly how the
organization is *really* behaving. As you and your organization grow, it can be

difficult to find the balance between letting go of too much too fast and holding on to too much for too long. But you must grow beyond this.

FEEL THIS: Seeing yourself as a bottleneck takes honest self-reflection. It's humbling and it's *hard*. Nobody wants to feel like they're the one creating problems in their own organization! Solving a problem that's *you* and not *who* is the hardest work you'll do, but it's worth it. In the end, no matter the outcome, the business—and you!—will be happier and healthier.

DO THIS: Take an honest look at how your organization is really functioning— not the published organizational chart. Are you or is another leader a bottleneck? Dig deep into why: Are the goals not clear, is the team not trustworthy or are you just too controlling? Keep talking with the team and digging in until you find the real answer; then take quick action to solve for this. Remember, by the time you have figured this out at the top, chances are people around you have been suffering for weeks or months.

Show me a CEO who has too many direct reports and I will show you a leader who is afraid to lose control or who doesn't truly trust his managers. When all decisions must run through one person, a weak decision-making culture prevails and the organization cannot scale. Empowering your leaders, on the other hand, creates success on many levels—for the CEO, the leadership team and the company as a whole.

When an organization is very small—ten employees or fewer— it may make sense for all decisions to go through the CEO. But if you have any ambitions to grow—or even to develop great leaders or managers internally—this structure is not sustainable.

Here's a quick exercise to see if you have this problem: Ask your leadership team to draw a very rough organization chart of how your organization *really* functions. If more than a few people draw something that looks like a rake, you have a problem.

A rake organization will never grow into a Level 3 business.

Let that sink in. Your business will *never* meet its full potential with this type of structure.

Are you single-handedly holding your company back, throttling it with your lack of trust and desire for control?

The unintended consequence of a rake organization is that it forces the CEO to become a manager. Most CEOs are technical geniuses, product gurus or incredible market builders, but they are usually lousy managers. Truth is, most CEOs don't have great day-to-day management skills—and even if they do, being a CEO should be more about *leadership* than about *management*. A rake organization actually forces very successful CEOs to start spending most of their time on their weakest suit—managing—and less time on their strengths. This may be due to lack of trust in the team, having the wrong people in managerial leadership positions or a host of other issues. (All of them are bad and most of them are other warning signs of success you should address.)

If you decide that you have a rake organization, a common response is to hire a manager to manage the other executives and make sure the trains run on time—someone to facilitate communications between the CEO and the rest of the team. Problem solved, right? Absolutely not. You've just moved your rake down a notch. This manager is usually someone who "deserves a chance" or doesn't really fit anywhere else in the organization, and hiring him for this position is almost always a disaster.

We've all seen this in family-owned businesses—the son-in-law or someone else with a similar last name "earns" this role. It goes back to the second warning sign, Bad Management of Great Opportunities; you can't fill a name in a box in your org chart before you have fully defined the role and understand the skills needed for it.

I am familiar with a successful, growing company owned by a charismatic man who fancied himself an expert—at everything. So he had his hands in everything: what advertisements should look like, which vendors he should buy from, which people or companies were deemed worthy of owning one of his franchises. He personally oversaw every aspect of the company and brought family members in—many of whom had zero work experience—to take on key roles once the actual professionals got fed up and quit. Of course, the family members were a protected class who could do no wrong—until he decided they did and fired them.

Soon the owner's legal bills from unhappy former franchisees and disgruntled employees outweighed the profits of his previously successful business. His leadership team was decimated—except for the ones related to him. He ended up losing all his franchisees, closing most of the stores and putting a black mark on the company's reputation for years to come. All because he insisted on making all decisions—large and small—himself.

He wanted everything and ended up with nothing.

In short, you can't have the organizational structure of a jellyfish—which is what a rake organization is—and expect to behave like a cheetah, which is what intense growth requires. Your Level 2 business—the stage when this warning sign of success most often appears—will never become a Level 3 firm with this organizational structure in place. It's impossible.

Warning Signs: How Do You Know If You're a Leadership Bottleneck?

Pay attention—really pay attention—to these warning signs. Do you see your situation here anywhere?

- Your organization chart looks like a rake, or there are dotted lines everywhere. Everything leads back to one or a few people.
- As CEO, you find yourself spending time on things that seem frivolous. If you really ask yourself, "Does this decision directly impact the core goals of this organization?" and it does not, you need someone else to worry about it—or eliminate it altogether.
- Your business is slowing because everyone is waiting on something from you.
- You have an endless list of tasks, and all of them are urgent.
- You feel that if it is going to get done right, you are going to have to do it yourself.
- You find that you or a few key people are the ones doing all the work, despite the fact that you are now paying others to do the work.
- Most, if not all, innovation and strategic thinking comes from you.
- Your executives are waiting on you to move forward, or if they do act independently, you circle back and undo what they have done.

Root Cause: Here's the *Real* Problem

So why is this happening? You can't move forward until you truly understand the root cause.

- For whatever reason, you don't trust the people on the executive team. If this is the case, you need to dig deeper: Is it because *you* can't let go, you have the *wrong people* in place or they're not *aligned* with the direction you're going? Get very clear on this.

- You have promoted people to a level of their incompetence. This goes back to the Bad Management of Great Opportunities, as well as Right Idea, Wrong Person. You have the wrong people in key roles. It's time to take a hard look at the job descriptions and requirements for these positions, separate from the people who are currently in those roles. This is easy to say but extremely difficult to do.
- You can't let go of decisions. If you want your business to grow, you must let go. Otherwise, learn to be happy with a Level 1 or Level 2 business—and there's nothing wrong with that. Determining you don't want to grow beyond a certain level can be freeing in itself. If you determine that's the case, though, it's time to be honest with yourself and the rest of your leadership team.

Problem Solving: Triage Your Current Situation

Soon you'll get out of problem-solving mode because you'll build your problem-predicting muscles—and you won't find yourself in this situation again. For now, though, you need quick solutions to get you out of this immediate situation.

- Apologize to your team. You have created a stressful environment where you expect fast growth, but you've created a human speed bump—yourself!—that nobody can avoid. Start here. This is the only way to have the open, honest conversations you need to solve this issue.
- Determine the real root cause or causes from the Root Cause list above—the causes, not just the symptoms.

Getting clarity here helps you solve the problem. Here are some keys to determining this:

- Do I have the right job descriptions for my leadership team, a real understanding of what their roles truly are?
- Do I let them own their roles and hold them accountable for results, and not micromanage how they get there (as long as they do it with integrity and within our core values)?
- Have I always secretly worried that nobody can do it as well as I can?

- If you've put another layer in place, you need to be honest about that person's skills and abilities. If you have just added another layer to your rake, this person is in a no-win situation.
- Once you get to the bottom of the issue, take action promptly. It's tough to make changes at the top. It's even tougher to say, "As CEO, I need to focus on X and only X. I'll stay out of my executives' way." The sooner you get to the bottom of the root causes of this problem, the faster your company can get back to growth. If you hesitate, you risk burning your executives out and missing huge opportunities for your business because you're so mired in this problem.

Problem Predicting: Build These Muscles to Avoid This Tough Situation in the Future

The real growth comes from surviving these situations, and then—instead of putting your head down until the next crisis—building processes and systems that prevent the problem from happening again.

To avoid Leadership Bottleneck in the future, go back to your organization chart. What are the core leadership needs for your type of business? What are the core skills and nonnegotiable traits needed for these positions? Take a hard look as you're interviewing people for those positions—lean on your effective hiring processes, learned in Right Idea, Wrong Person. Take the time to hire the right people into the right roles from the beginning, and hold them accountable long after the interview is over.

Be humble and smart enough to hire people who are smarter than you. As leaders, we all say we do this, but do we really? Truth is, you can't possibly be an expert at everything—you must surround yourself with people who blow you away with their insights and fresh perspectives every day. Not only are you creating a brighter future for yourself and your organization, but you're also helping create a great leader who will go on to do great things—in your organization or beyond. *Nothing is more fulfilling to a real leader than to foster growth in others.*

Even the best leaders get mired in their own control issues. Not even the CEO of a Fortune 500 company was insulated from this warning sign of success. He hired senior executives from Apple—the best and brightest rock stars. But then he proceeded to tell everyone what to do, how to do it and what the priorities were. The team rebelled: "Hey, listen, if you're gonna make all the decisions, we'll go back to Apple. You clearly don't need anyone this senior." He'd surrounded himself with the best but wouldn't or couldn't let them do what they did best.

As the saying goes, you alone can do it but you cannot do it alone. The fact is, if you and your organization are going to grow you are going to have to hire the right people and let them do their jobs. Yes, as the leader of your team you get to be (and should be) the ultimate tiebreaker. However, if the tie always goes in your favor, expect talented people to leave and make way for mediocre people to join your team, the ones who are OK with you always being right. Learn to expand your capacity with the help of others and watch your business expand as a result.

Twitter CEO Dick Costolo shared the following anecdote in "Dick Costolo and Ben Horowitz on the Give and Take of Taking the Reins" about being a "junior" leader in the room with a more senior team.

> "You don't want to too frequently say, 'Okay, I hear what you guys are saying but we're gonna do A'—because then [leadership team members] start to tune out," he says. "So I try to make sure that even if I go into the room disagreeing with these guys, if I start to hear from a bunch of senior people that 'We really feel A and we feel about it this way,' I'll set my thinking aside and say, 'All right, let's go do that.' And then I have to leave the room and commit to that decision. I can't say later if they were wrong, 'Well, I thought Y but those guys wanted to do X.' There's no better way to undermine your own leadership."[2]

In the same article, Ben Horowitz, general partner at venture capital firm Andreessen Horowitz, talked about his experience of knowing when it's clear the CEO needs help:

> A lot of people want the guy who gets the trains to run on time; it's like, let's get somebody who's a real, professional manager—a been-there, done-that guy.
>
> Those people don't tend to work out that well because they'll often shove the founder to the side and seek to put their own imprint on the company without the knowledge or the moral authority. What generally happens is they'll maximize so it will all be great until you need a new product—and then the company dies.[3]

"Managing by trying to be liked is the path to ruin," says Twitter CEO Dick Costolo. Horowitz adds, "Nobody is actually a natural CEO. You learn the job, and the job is hard and weird and awkward and unnatural."[4]

Above all, being a CEO means you must be honest with yourself and your team, no matter the cost. It's incredibly humbling.

So What? Now What?

Admitting that you're a bottleneck in your own organization is humbling. Solving this problem requires you to let go of your ego, admit to your shortcomings, ask your team for help—and actually trust their leadership—and create an organization that plays to everyone's strengths.

Remember, the road to heaven does go through hell . . . and it's worth it. You can decide if it will be a day trip or a daily trip.

THE FIFTH WARNING SIGN OF SUCCESS: **HOPE IS NOT A STRATEGY**

KNOW THIS: Creating a strategic plan is not easy, but setting clear goals, then working backward to get to today's plan makes everything easier. Too often as leaders we get so focused on the product (in this case, a strategic plan) that we shortcut and undervalue the process. Experience has taught me that the plan can be useless, but the process is priceless!

FEEL THIS: Creating a strategic plan feels overwhelming. Even the best leaders find it difficult to take a step back and invest the time to create a living strategic plan. Do not spend time worrying if you have the absolute right plan; trust me, every great leader worries. Your plan will not be perfect, but if you have a process that identifies the right three to five goals and keeps measuring progress throughout the year, the imperfections will get corrected.

Strategic planning does work; if it is not working for you, then you either have a poor process or the wrong team to execute it.

DO THIS: Stop the madness. Take some time to work with your team to create a highly efficient and effective process that identifies three to five specific goals, and then prioritize ruthlessly to reach them. Focus on doing less and concentrating only on what will really help you get there. Get help if you need it, but listen to your intuition: If you feel that whoever is helping you is simply making things more complex and drawn out, get away from them fast! Do not be fooled by their credentials or company name. Ask them about how they would go about helping you and your teams develop a living strategic plan, and listen to your gut. You may not know how to do it, but I bet you know a good idea versus a bad idea when you hear it. Trust yourself!

You and your team have a huge opportunity in front of you. You may have multiple all-day meetings in beautiful locations and develop what you think is a fantastic strategic plan. People are energized; there are countless action items and perhaps even binders full of notes that capture all the great ideas. You and your team assume your clarity will transfer to everyone in the organization, or maybe you have a company-wide meeting to share all that occurred during your hours of planning.

And then you *hope* it all goes as planned.

You think, "If we sell X units, everything will be okay." But then, as the days melt into weeks and the weeks melt into months, you realize you're not getting there. Your notebook of great ideas gathers dust. You're frustrated, your team is getting burned-out and you're not sure how to move forward.

What happened to all that exciting momentum?

Fact is, there's a huge difference between stating a goal and knowing how to reach it. Simply working hard, putting in a lot of hours or hitting a "magic" sales number doesn't get you where you need to be. You must first take the overly obvious and embarrassingly *simple*—but *not easy!*—step of clearly defining your real goals, then breaking them down to determine your precise next steps.

You must have a *simple* and *measurable* communication document that you can hand anyone that clearly explains

1. The company's three to five goals
2. What will be different one year from now if you meet these goals
3. What measurable objectives will be apparent each quarter
4. The first actions that need to be initiated for each goal

Remember my story from earlier in the book: I worked with a company that specialized in a highly technical field creating "clean room" technology needed to house supercompressor computers. Then one day, one of the leaders decided they should invest in . . . a trailer park. It nearly bankrupted their company and certainly derailed their success for a number of months, which they spent dealing with the fallout from an unwise—and unrelated—diversification product. If they had had a strategic plan in place, the answer to this "opportunity" would have been a short, simple "no" in the boardroom, because it simply wouldn't have fit into their strategic plan. Think of the money, energy, time and heartache they would have saved.

Haven't we all been in this position? We should have done the *right* thing and said no, but we weren't brave enough or couldn't put our finger on why it wasn't right. A strategic plan gives you a clear road map—for today, next quarter and years from now. You'll know exactly where you are—and where you should be—all along the journey.

Warning Signs: How Do You Know If You're Counting on Hope as Your Strategy?

Pay attention—really pay attention—to these warning signs. Do you see yourself in here anywhere?

- You think you have a long-term strategy in place, but you keep hearing, "We are not sure where we are going," or the goals aren't being met, and people are floundering.
- When asked, most people in your company cannot tell you the three to five goals/focus areas.
- You find yourself hoping that the hard work, long hours and stress you and your leadership team put into the business will create a successful, sustainable business— even if you doubt that anything is actually being accomplished.
- Your strategic planning process produces a lot of great ideas, but vague next steps and a lack of accountability cause the actual implementation to stall.
- Your leadership team doesn't present a united front, so the company isn't sure what to focus on.
- Your employees cannot confidently state what winning looks like in their area of responsibility.
- Leaders do not know how or when to say no, so they say yes to too many things, causing the organization to lose focus or be led into a fog.
- When you state your audacious goals to the team, they say they don't believe they can get there; the job is too big, you don't have enough resources or it feels impossible.
- The company rewards busywork instead of results.
- As the business grows and becomes more complex, confusion and frustration permeate the organization.

- When you ask midlevel employees how their work helps move company goals forward, they don't know how to answer you. They either don't know the goals or they don't understand how their specific work impacts the bigger picture.

Root Cause: Here's the *Real* Problem

So why is this happening? You can't move forward until you truly understand the root cause.

- When "hope" is the only strategy, it means that there's no *real* strategic plan in place. Although no one would admit that "hope" is the strategy, play back the tape and be honest: The results do not lie. You need a strategic plan that's truly focused and measurable, that everyone understands and that predicts the problems before they appear in the business. Effective strategic plans reflect organizational discipline, accountability and direction. They are active, articulate, and well communicated and can be created only by a strong, experienced leadership team.
- The lack of a true plan creates stress and burnout among your team. You don't want to lose talented people because you haven't taken the time to create a plan so you and your team can prioritize and work hard on the *right* things, not *everything.*

Problem Solving: Triage Your Current Situation

Soon you'll get out of problem-solving mode because you'll build your problem-predicting muscles—and you won't find yourself in this situation again. For now, though, you need quick solutions to get you out of this immediate situation.

You must make creating an annual strategic planning process your top priority—now. There are many models available to help you create a robust, measurable plan, so choose the simplest, least intimidating model and get started.

How do you know if your strategic plan is solid?

1. It includes a 50,000-foot view, including the goals you are committed to reach in the next few years. This should consist of three to five goals; they can be abstract at this level.
2. It then goes to your objectives for the coming 12 months. If we were wildly successful, what would we see one year from now?
3. Performance metrics are in place for each quarter. How do you measure the goals you've set? What does each team member or department contribute to the goals, and how do you know if you're getting there? Metrics and measurement are key here.
4. Finally, your plan includes key actions for the next 30, 60 or 90 days. What are the very next steps you should take to move forward on your quarterly goals?
5. The plan is reviewed and updated continuously, and team members review and measure their role in the plan regularly, if not daily. Yes, daily!

The plan may take several days (spread over a couple of months) of intensive work to create; however, the end result must be simple. If it doesn't fit onto one page, it's too complex. That does not mean there are not reams of paper with backup. You must be able to boil this document down to the essentials, something that each employee can understand, a scenario where all employees can see where they fit in.

Once the plan is "complete," it is time to set up a regular review (at least once a quarter) of the plan and its components. It is *normal* to adjust and tweak the methods to achieve the goals based on better information you get throughout the year. It is *not normal* to change the 50,000-foot goals every quarter.

I get it—it feels daunting to try to "stop" and build a strategic plan right now, in the midst of growth or confusion or even a crisis. But I promise you—I've seen it time and again—your problems will only get worse if you don't truly commit to creating and executing a plan now. Remember, we get what we set ourselves up for. Here it is again . . . the road to heaven does go through hell . . . it is your choice if it is a day trip or a daily trip!

Problem Predicting: Build These Muscles to Avoid This Tough Situation in the Future

The real growth comes from surviving these situations, and then—instead of putting your head down until the next crisis—building processes and systems that prevent the problem from happening again.

Once you have a strategic plan in place, you'll wonder how you ever got anything done without it. The plan becomes your true north, helping you stay the course when a crisis hits. A strategic plan provides:

- *A unified direction for your company.* A strategic plan is a valuable leadership device. Employees can sense when the organization is focused—and when it's muddied. Chances are, competitors can see it, too.
- *Better anticipation of risks.* Effective planning means that most risks are considered and discussed in advance, and

contingency plans are built. For example, you wouldn't "risk" investing in a trailer park.

- *A heightened sense of order and discipline.* Clear targets, frequent measurement and positive feedback create accountability and focus.

- *More effective communication.* This clear direction improves communications with employees, customers and creditors.

- *Improved leadership and management skills.* An effective strategic facilitator will help all managers understand what to do and why.

- *A strengthened sense of commitment.* As planning team members, key managers gain a high sense of commitment to making the planned results happen. This commitment is much stronger than when a plan is developed by others and handed to the managers for execution.

So What? Now What?

It's time to rise above the chaos and crisis and dig into planning. I've helped organizations create a strategic plan on just one 8.5 x 11-inch sheet of paper, using the four steps outlined above. It's simple—but not easy—to get clear about your goals, and doing so really will help to solve almost all the warning signs of success you're seeing in your organization.

EIGHT

CULTURE

THE NEXT FOUR WARNING SIGNS OF SUCCESS

NEITHER SUCCESS NOR FAILURE HAPPENS IN A VACUUM. TO examine why you're not succeeding, or not succeeding fast enough, or succeeding but too quickly for you to scale, look first to the organization and ask, "Where is your culture taking you?"

That's exactly what we'll be doing as we examine and drill deeper into the next four warning signs of success.

THE SIXTH WARNING SIGN OF SUCCESS: **CORE VALUES MELTDOWN**

KNOW THIS: You created core values for your company for a reason: because they matter. Think of all the companies (and people) who got off track because they lost sight of, negotiated away, compromised or really never believed their core values.

FEEL THIS: When you're not being true to your core values, you can feel it in your gut. Pay attention to this feeling; it's real, and it's there for a reason.

> **DO THIS:** Review—and I mean really, actually read—your core values each week if you think you're getting off track. Dig into *what* compromises you're making to uncover *why* you feel you need to make them. Continue to challenge leadership and team members to review and stay true to the core values, especially and particularly when you're going through a crisis. These core values can keep you going.

A Core Values Meltdown may show itself in a crisis, but it can simmer below the surface for a long time. Keeping values front and center at your organization helps ensure that they permeate all levels of the organization and become its foundation.

There is nothing more miserable than being led by someone with inconsistent values. I have seen this warning sign of success single-handedly take an organization down. The interesting thing is that everyone saw it happening, and very few did anything about it, but when it was all over, everyone clearly blamed a subtle whitewashing of the company's founding values over a long period of time.

How do such core values, initially nonnegotiable, break down? In most cases, the pressures of rapid growth force small compromises, each of which is like a tiny fissure in the bedrock of the company. Exceptions are made for special circumstances, brilliant jerks are tolerated and your team members start to question whether those founding values really meant anything. Frustrated managers and employees—particularly long-timers—create an "us versus them" environment as things change. It's simple—but not easy—to keep focused on core values, but it takes practice and unwavering commitment.

I worked with a company where a CEO hired a stellar, well-known executive from a large, well-known company he had once worked for himself. The terms of his own exit from the previous company required that he not poach people. But he needed a vice president and, guess what? The "perfect" (which usually means little more than "convenient") candidate worked there. So he created a loophole, having the new VP report to another executive so it didn't look like he had poached.

It seemed like a small compromise, even though one of the core, critical values of this company was authenticity. Transparency was key to the business and to the culture, and clearly the executive wasn't acting transparently.

But it wasn't until almost a year later, when the executive's whole team was unhappy and in disarray, goals weren't being met, spending was out of control and 30% of the team members had quit, that it became obvious that this executive was very problematic.

The CEO, as humans do, saw only the data necessary to support the perception he wanted to have: that this man was on the up-and-up; that the years of experience he brought to the company meant that he would fit into and value the long-established culture—including authenticity. But the reality was radically different. Balanced leadership includes building both people and performance, and valuing them equally (see figure 16, "Dando Leadership Style Matrix"). If your values are out of balance, the consequences can be unsettling.

Too often we talk about values in relation to how *we* behave, but true leadership demands that we combine behaviors *and* performance to collectively embody these values.

Warning Signs: How Do You Know If You or Your Team Is Having a Core Values Meltdown?

Pay attention—really pay attention—to these warning signs. Do you see your situation here anywhere?

Dando Leadership Style Matrix

Balanced Leadership Builds Culture AND the Bottom Line

Some of us stay focused on culture, employee satisfaction and relationships when it comes to leading teams. Others want results, and focus purely on job performance to ensure company success. The world's best leaders know their personal limitations and achieve the necessary balance through other people.

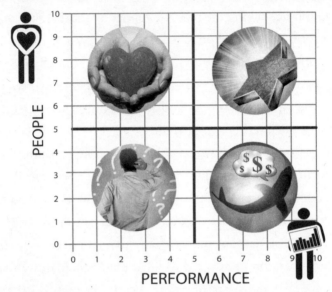

 You've got the heart, but you might need more head in the game.

 You may think you're leading, but it is probably time to turn around to see if anyone is following.

 Leadership is in your DNA. The balance between people & performance is at the heart of your success.

 The bottom line tops your list. It's probably time to bring people closer to the top of your priority list.

What Is Your Leadership Style?

Map the coordinates on the Dando Leadership Style Matrix by rating yourself from 1 to 10 in the categories of people and performance.

1) Start with the people side of the chart first. Move your finger up the left side of the chart and stop on the number that you feel fits your aptitude for people leadership (note that 1 is lowest and 10 is highest).

2) Now rate yourself from 1 to 10 on the performance side. Map the coordinates by connecting the placement of the vertical and horizontal lines.

You may want to have your team, board members, etc. fill this out on your behalf. This is a great way to address the gaps that can hold you back.

Figure 16

- You feel you can't be honest or open about some of the activities you're doing.
- Not everyone in the organization can clearly and passionately express the values of the organization and cite examples of them in action.
- You have a team of people who like to play "gotcha" and point out shortcomings, rather than helping one another better embody the company values.
- You have too many words to describe a few simple concepts.
- You do not have any values based in performance because it feels too "corporate," yet you expect team members to perform like cheetahs.
- You know some employees are acting in ways that are not aboveboard, but you're avoiding confrontation.
- Employees are reticent to give feedback about their managers or the executive team. You see a lot of closed-door meetings.

Compromises end up making simple things more complicated; it's always harder to keep track of lies than to keep track of the business.

Root Cause: Here's the *Real* Problem

So why is this happening? When you get to the root cause—the "why"—you can take effective action. This takes focused thinking and honest conversations. But you can't move forward until you truly understand the root cause.

- You do not take values into consideration when you are hiring or promoting team members, and now you have a team of skilled people with different values than the organization's. You and/or someone on your team is trying, unsuccessfully, to square the circle.

- Your values aren't clearly defined, so your team doesn't know precisely how they should be reflected in the business. You need to give vivid examples that relate directly to the daily activities of the business.

- You understand your values, but you can't point to clear examples of them at work every day in your business.

- You haven't done an honest review of your values in relation to your business recently, due to competing priorities. (The irony is, once you get clear on values, it makes other decisions easier.)

- You have great conversations about values at the executive level, but there's no implementation plan for instilling your values across the organization.

- You do not make your values part of your formal and informal review process. If you want to make something better, you must measure it and focus on it, systematically and regularly.

Problem Solving: Triage Your Current Situation

Soon you'll get out of problem-solving mode because you'll build your problem-predicting muscles—and you won't find yourself in this situation again. For now, though, you need quick solutions to get you out of your immediate situation. Remember: We get what we set ourselves up for. Take a moment to honestly assess where you are right now, so you can move ahead with purpose.

- Take time to acknowledge with your entire team, all at once, that you are experiencing a core values meltdown. Review your values and explain how they drive the business.

- Core values shouldn't change, but they can evolve. Talk about any perceived gaps between the stated values and the day-to-day reality, and brainstorm examples of what's going wrong—and right.

- Encourage all managers to conduct the same exercise with their teams, to clarify how each team, in all that they do, should reinforce the values.

- Brainstorm ways across the organization to reinforce the values. Make sure to engage all types of employees here; it's easy to feel like values are vapid corporate-speak. Ask employees to share how they embody and embrace the values each day.

Problem Predicting: Build These Muscles to Avoid This Tough Situation in the Future

The real growth comes from surviving these situations, and then—instead of putting your head down until the next crisis—building processes and systems that prevent the problem from happening again. *If you take your team out of problem-solving mode, they'll use their brain cells to innovate and move the business forward—where you want it to go.*

I've found that the best companies have *all three* of these basic components:

1. The *skeleton* is the organizational structure of the company and determines how the organization functions. Like I have said, it is very difficult for a company to have the structure of a jellyfish yet behave like a cheetah. Sadly, many companies think they have the organizational structure of a cheetah, but in reality, they have the structure of a rake (one dominant leader with a bunch of people reporting to him or her).

2. The *central nervous system* includes the systems that create consistent and predictable outcomes for a company.

As the saying goes, if you do not design the systems, they will design themselves, often very poorly.

3. The *soul* of a company includes the invisible, but very real elements: the *nonnegotiable* vision, core values, and goals put upon it daily by the actions, behaviors and passions of the people who created and work at the company. The soul of a company is the most significant way for leaders and their teams both to positively influence the bottom line *and* to truly make a significant contribution toward making the world a better place—if their actions are authentic.

With this in mind, here are some ways to ensure that you don't fall into another crisis:

- Keep values on the agenda of regular executive meetings. Include values conversations in major decisions.
- Hire people whose values match the organization's; do not expect people to change just to collect a paycheck. Sure, most people will claim to accept the values in an interview setting, but we all show our true colors when we're under pressure.
- Beware of compromises. Values themselves shouldn't change, but how they play out will inevitably evolve. For example, when you're starting up, "openness" means that anyone can walk in and talk directly to the CEO. When you get much bigger, and it's difficult to have the same level of access to the CEO, does this mean that "openness" is no longer possible? Or does it just mean that the CEO has put competent leadership in place to handle many issues?

Too many times, I have seen teams who've felt they lost a value. But often, it is not lost; it's just expressed differently as the company grows. Make no mistake: Telling the truth, or doing what we say we will do, does not change, but the environments do. We must prepare for our own success.

- When you consider values as part of every conversation you have and every decision you make, it becomes second nature—but it takes repetition to build a habit until it's innate.
- If you think about priorities as your true north, think of values as home base. Values are where you lay your head at night, where you're comfortable and sure. In the face of chaos, growth or crisis, you can always look to your values to ensure you're heading in the right direction.

So What? Now What?

A Core Values Meltdown can show itself in a crisis, but it can be simmering below the surface for a long time—especially if you don't face it head-on from the beginning. Keeping values front and center as the foundation of day-to-day life at your organization helps ensure that they permeate all levels of the organization, so they become muscle memory.

Remember what I said, and think about your own personal experiences. There is nothing more miserable or demoralizing than being led by someone who has no consistent values.

THE SEVENTH WARNING SIGN OF SUCCESS:
DRINKING THE CHAOS KOOL-AID

KNOW THIS: Unlimited potential and opportunities exist (literally) everywhere. The power comes from focusing on not only the *right* things but also only a *few* things and making them *great*. Great strategy is about not just figuring out the 5% you will do but figuring out the 95% you will not do.

FEEL THIS: When you're in charge of an organization or team, you feel obligated to make the most of everything—to make the company excel everywhere, exceed all expectations. Sometimes the path forward is not clear but the consequences of getting it wrong are very clear. So you and your team say yes to everything. This feels safe: You feel like you have not missed any options. However, this creates a strategy that is a mile wide and an inch deep. If you have a scattered focus, you will get scattered results. Fact is, it's possible to do only a few things exceptionally well.

DO THIS: Acknowledge the potential, and acknowledge that it's possible to reach all of it—but realize you can't do it all at once. Take a moment to remember your primary, overriding goals—refer back to your mission, vision and strategic plan—to help guide your next move. You must build and exercise your leadership muscles, which help you build on and execute the right *priorities.* Learn when to say yes and when to say no.

Your business keeps you energized. You see potential in new products, new markets—there's opportunity everywhere. The thrill of so much activity impedes your ability to say no, or perhaps you don't have systems in place to reveal how to actually spend your limited resources (time and money). It all adds up to chaos, but it doesn't have to.

Your company is doing well. You started up with little or nothing, and you've grown to a size or reputation that you never thought possible—at least not so quickly. In any case, you're more excited than ever. You've hired a great team, and everything is bumping along.

When you start to see the next level of your business, there's so much opportunity! "The market is ripe for the taking in growth opportunities around the world—we've got to get there! Our customers are clamoring for more products to buy from us—why don't we have anything new yet this year? Our investors are bullish on our growth!"

Wow. So much forward motion is incredible. Energizing. Fun! Your team is busy, people have creative ideas, and you're having the time of your life.

Until something changes. There's a new competitor—could they overtake us? China is great, but what about Latin America? The economy is changing; should we slow our growth? The leadership team is working long hours on a variety of initiatives and you start to wonder if all (or *any*) of them are going to help you meet your strategic goals. (Are you still tracking those, day by day, quarter by quarter?) You quietly wonder if you have the right goals in place—and the right metrics to know if you're reaching those goals.

So a new set of "priorities" is put in place. Your nimble team pivots to the challenge. China's still important, but the business development team adds Brazil to the list. The growth may not happen as quickly, but let's start a massive search for a new CFO and COO anyway. Maybe that competitor has the right idea— let's add more features to our next product release.

You can see where this is going; I'm exhausted just thinking about it. The team trusts and listens to you, so they say "yes!" to everything too. But over time, you'll realize that the company isn't really living up to its fullest potential. Sure, you meet the product launch date, but was the functionality as good as it could have been? Is global expansion the right thing to do right now?

Did you invest in a trailer park?

Too often, I've seen high-growth companies stop being high-growth companies by mistaking busyness for accomplishment. It may be a great sign of dedication that your engineering team stays up all night to meet a goal, but it also suggests that they can't get it done within a reasonable amount of time—so it may not be a reasonable request. It feels great to say "yes!" to everything, to build something new, to tread new ground. And it feels terrible to say no. Sure, it takes courage to say yes, but sometimes saying no can be even more energizing, because it gives you the freedom and clarity to do what is truly most important.

Real strategy is not just determining the 5% you will do. It is also figuring out the 95% you won't. (Remember the trailer park. And remember the whole reason you created your strategic plan: to stay focused on your highest and best calling as a company.)

At its very core, Drinking the Chaos Kool-Aid happens because *everyone in your company* does not understand—deeply understand—and buy into the goals of your business and *how* the goals will specifically be achieved. There cannot be more than a few core goals, because there's really no such thing as scattered focus. If you haven't set clear, measurable goals for your organization, it's time to do that. Go back a step and create your strategic plan. Determine the precise metrics that will help you understand if you are reaching your goals. Then think carefully about the exact strategies that will help you get there.

It's as simple—but not easy!—as that. If you or a team member comes up with a seemingly great new idea, resist the urge to jump at it until you've asked, "Does this help us meet our goals?"

Experience has taught me that there are three types of leaders who value the importance of clearly defining their company goals, getting their teams aligned to those goals and keeping them focused:

1. *The Lucky Leaders.* These are the leaders who have the natural inclination to lead a team and keep them focused. It may be a function of their genetics, their upbringing or both.

2. *Leaders Standing on Scars.* These leaders learned their lessons the hard way—in some cases, it was *very hard.* There are precisely two reasons we change: We create a crisis or we have a crisis. These leaders had a crisis.

3. *Leaders Who Do Not Know What They Do Not Know.* These are Standing on Scars leaders in training. If you asked these leaders if they think goals, focus and measurement are important, they will be offended that you could ask them such a stupid question . . . Yes! However, if you asked every person in their organization to tell you the company goals, how they impact those goals on a daily basis and how they are measured, fewer than 40% of the people in the company could answer the question.

Like many other warning signs of success, Drinking the Chaos Kool-Aid is a surefire way to exhaust yourself, run off team members, and turn your passion into dread. You can destroy your organization by focusing on busyness over the real business you are in.

It's also a clear indication that you don't have clarity around the three to five measurable goals of the business. I cannot overstate that, once your goals are clear, it's actually simple—not easy, but simple—to understand precisely where to focus.

Warning Signs: How Do You Know If You or Your Team Is Drinking the Chaos Kool-Aid?

Pay attention—really pay attention—to these warning signs. Do you see your situation here anywhere?

- Your team tells you that the atmosphere feels chaotic.

- You see a lot of activity—the team is exhausted and busy—but you can't see the results.
- "Scattered results" from figure 7 in chapter 4 really speaks to you.
- Meetings take too long, get emotional and yield few tangible results. The list of company goals keeps getting longer.
- Your business's or unit's performance is not what you think it should be.
- Key strategies and goals constantly change . . . for a variety of reasons.
- Customer and employee feedback suggests that no one is sure what the company stands for anymore.

If you are not sure if you are Drinking the Chaos Kool-Aid, at your next leadership meeting have everyone take out a piece of paper and ask them to answer the following (no discussion, just writing):

1. List the three to five goals of the company for this year and the coming year.
2. Give at least one or two examples for each goal of how the company will measure and know it has achieved the goal six months from now and one year from now.
3. Do you review your plan and use the goals and measurements to plan your time on *a daily basis?*
4. Do you think there is anyone on the team who cannot answer the first three questions? (Just answer yes or no; specific names are not needed.)

The answers to these four questions will tell you if you are Drinking the Chaos Kool-Aid. You're not looking for someone to parrot back canned answers; you want to know whether they get the essence of what is trying to be accomplished.

Root Cause: Here's the *Real* Problem

So why is this happening? You can't move forward until you truly understand the root cause.

- You either don't have clear goals or you don't know how to effectively measure them. Without this true north, you cannot determine what to do or—more important—what *not* to do.
- Your company is truly on the path of greatness, and you're thinking correctly about all the possibilities, but you lack the focus to execute.
- You're not clear about your priorities, or you're not keeping them in mind every day, applying them to every— and I mean *every*—decision you make.

Problem Solving: Triage Your Current Situation

Soon you'll get out of problem-solving mode because you'll build your problem-predicting muscles—and you won't find yourself in this situation again. For now, though, you need quick solutions to get you out of this immediate situation.

- Take time to acknowledge the chaos with your entire team, all at once. Show that you understand the chaos and why it's there, and explain that you must all work together to get focused.
- If your company does not have a strategic plan that gets and keeps everyone laser focused, then guess what? You need one. I get that you're cynical; most people spend zero time on planning or they make it complicated and spend too much time filling pages and pages with a dizzying

amount of unnecessary detail. The problem is not with the *idea* of creating and executing a strategic plan; it is most often with the *people* creating the plan. An active, articulate, well-communicated direction for a corporation, division or business unit is evidence of leadership. Effective strategic plans encompass organizational discipline, accountability and direction. (See the fifth warning sign of success, Hope Is Not a Strategy, for more context.)

- Review the company's key priorities with the team. Do you all agree that these are still your priorities? Resist, at all costs, the urge to keep adding priorities—something has to give. Decide which priorities should be de-emphasized so you can focus on something else. And explore why that change wouldn't have come up in prior planning. You need to dig deep into what's really happening here.

- Once priorities are reviewed or updated, look at what each team is doing. What is taking up all their time and energy? Are these activities the *right* activities? If not, prioritize brutally. Your rock star employees—I promise you—will be thrilled with the accountability and focus this brings to their daily work lives. They can finally ditch the boring busywork and surprise you with how quickly they find ways to meet or beat the goals.

- Center again on your goals, metrics and instrumentation to track success, so you make informed decisions.

- Keep a close eye on "chaos creep." If you or anyone on the team starts to stray outside the core goals, point it out and talk about it. Maybe the core goals should change. Or maybe the effort should be tabled until the big rocks get moved.

- Make sure *everyone* in your company can easily answer the four questions in the Warning Signs section.

Problem Predicting: Build These Muscles to
Avoid This Tough Situation in the Future

The real growth comes from surviving these situations, and then—instead of putting your head down until the next crisis—building processes and systems that prevent the problem from happening again.

- Think and talk about how and why chaos could creep into your company. Decide whether you are all aligned on your core company goals, or if they should change. Alternatively, should the members of the team change?
- Develop (do not just write) a strategic plan that gets and keeps everyone—yes, *everyone*—laser focused.
- Think about your business as a journey or a long train ride. Every turn should take you closer to your destination. Sometimes you need a pit stop, a break. Sometimes you need to stop to tune up the engine. But if you stray from your route too long or get off course, you'll never get to your destination. Worse yet, your destination—your organization's true potential—may be gone by the time you get there.
- Acknowledge a great idea every single time it surfaces. You are not punishing yourself or anyone on the team for great ideas. Actually, you should have a robust and simple process for generating as many ideas as possible around your core goals, about how to make them happen faster and better. But you absolutely must base all your *actions* on your core priorities—in order to succeed. This means not every idea—good or bad—will make it into the business plan.

So What? Now What?

Drinking the Chaos Kool-Aid can take over a team gradually or quickly, but in any case, it's a signal of poor leadership and distractions that can sap your team's energy or derail your business permanently.

When faced with a new idea or decision, ask yourself and your team, "Is this the highest and best use of our time and resources to meet our goal?" Be honest and open to the answer.

THE EIGHTH WARNING SIGN OF SUCCESS:
COMMUNICATION VACUUM (AKA, IT SUCKS!)

KNOW THIS: Communication problems are typically a red herring or a symptom of something bigger; you have to dig to get to the real issue. Almost every organization I know has identified "poor communication" as a key issue. If you take this bait, there is a company newsletter or some other expensive internal communication vehicle in your future. Most likely, it won't solve the "poor communication" problem.

FEEL THIS: Communication is difficult in all important relationships, not just business. When we feel like we're not being heard, it's demoralizing and hurtful. But you must take emotion and fear out of the equation to get to the core issues blocking communication.

DO THIS: Take an honest look at communication in your organization. Take notice where most critical communication happens in any company: meetings. See this warning sign of success for a game-changing way to improve where most critical communications happen. It is not intuitively obvious, but the key to great communication is not just talking or doing more of it; the key to great communication is *listening.*

Despite countless emails, newsletters and meetings, employees consistently identify poor communication as a core problem. As your company grows, senior managers have fewer day-to-day interactions with operations and hands-on team members, so communication falters in both directions. Executives feel out of touch, and employees feel ignored by those at the top. Learn how to communicate clearly and regularly about what's truly most important.

"Communication sucks!" is a common refrain I hear when I talk to employees. I always continue to question people when they bring this up: What do they need to know that they don't know? Is it really a lack of communication, or do employees actually not trust the leadership team? Do they not understand how their specific job fits into the company's overall goals?

When communication is lacking or unclear, rumors run rampant. If executives are arguing in the boardroom every week, people can tell something's amiss just by walking past. All you need is for one person to say, "I heard Joe yelling at Helen during the executive meeting," and the story is already beyond your control.

In the absence of official communication channels, team members will create their own, so it's critical to get in front of your firm's communication deficiencies. I get it: You can't air all your dirty laundry—nor should you! And not every member of the team needs to know everything that's going on at the executive level. But it's critical that core strategic goals, the specific ways you will get there and exactly how you will measure your success are clearly and regularly communicated. When you're already having conversations about what's truly important, it leads to more of the right conversations and to fewer rumors fueled by uncertainty.

Warning Signs: How Do You Know If Communication Sucks in Your Organization?

Pay attention—really pay attention—to these warning signs. Do you see yourself in here anywhere?

- You have so many meetings that people start to opt out of them because they're invited to too many. Or they physically attend but actually take mental field trips during the meeting.
- You wonder why you spend so much time in meetings, or you wonder why you're meeting so often.
- Employee surveys continuously pinpoint communication as a problem.
- When you ask midlevel employees how their daily work impacts the company's strategic goals, do they know the answer? If not, don't necessarily blame the employees—it could be that the information is just not communicated clearly.
- You have spent money and resources on an internal company newsletter, but no one seems to read it. Even though you put a secret code somewhere in the newsletter that allows them to win something.
- The key leaders in the business no longer get *the benefit of the doubt* from the rest of the company. Employees don't trust the leaders, so they use the word "communication" to describe the problem.
- *Even you* are not entirely clear about how each department contributes to the company's strategic goals.

Root Cause: Here's the *Real* Problem

So why is this happening? You can't move forward until you truly understand the root cause.

- You and/or your team are not clear about the direction of the company. This confusion transfers into the organization and is labeled "poor communication."

- You and/or your team have lost the benefit of the doubt.
- You have an honesty and transparency problem somewhere in the leadership team.
- Your strategic plan hasn't been clearly communicated to the entire organization. Employees don't understand specifically how their work fits into the company's overall goals, so it causes discomfort or lack of trust. This most often surfaces as "poor communication," though the real problem may be that the plan isn't strategic enough or hasn't been clearly shared across the organization. And this communication of the strategic plan to the individuals in your company doesn't best happen in one huge mandatory meeting. To really come alive to team members, it must be communicated one on one by direct managers. This means you and your leadership team must communicate the goals often, to various audiences in the company, and you must empower and train your managers to have these conversations with individual team members.

Problem Solving: Triage Your Current Situation

Soon you'll get out of problem-solving mode because you'll build your problem-predicting muscles—and you won't find yourself in this situation again. For now, though, you need quick solutions to get you out of this immediate situation.

Companies often say that meetings are out of control, they go nowhere, and there are too many of them. I've found that simply improving meetings gives companies the best return on investment for improving communication. My strategy for tackling meeting overload is overly obvious and embarrassingly simple.

You'll be tempted to ignore it, but I can tell you for certain that the main difference between successful leaders and unsuccessful leaders boils down to simply *taking action,* even on the simplest things. This process does, however, require an environment of honesty, where team members can share their opinions without condemnation. You're basically asking team members to give each meeting a grade, share the grade, then work to improve the meeting.

1. Have your team figure out how much time they spend in internal meetings each week and multiply that number by 52. You'll come up with the number of hours spent in meetings in a year, on average.

2. Have each of them figure their approximate hourly rate. If you're salaried, take your gross salary and divide it by 2,080 hours to determine this hourly rate.

3. Add up the hourly rate and multiply it by all the hours to determine your hard costs—just in salaries!—for meetings each year. Remember, this doesn't even take lost opportunities into account; think of everything else that could be accomplished with this time.

4. Work with your team to create a list of what makes a meeting extremely successful. Examples include an agenda, people come prepared, starts and ends on time, is a good use of time, and so on.

5. Have them select the two or three *most important* items from the list. If you did *only* these things, your meetings would be a great use of time, money and talent.

6. To create a baseline, have your team grade your regular meetings based on those top two or three criteria. Take the average of everyone's score and let that be your starting point. If you want, you can score different types of meetings, such as staff meetings, strategic planning meetings, project-specific meetings and so on.

7. Look at your annual investment from time spent in meetings from item 3 versus the average grade you just came up with in item 6. Are you satisfied with this grade? "One of my clients—I'll call him John Day—and his company followed this process, and originally their meetings had an average grade of 5.9 on a $2.3 million annual meeting investment. That is a failing grade and a huge waste, in anyone's book. Over a year's time their meetings' average grade went from 5.9 to 8.8, and they had the biggest revenue and profit year in their 35-year history. John said this overly obvious, embarassingly simple but not easy idea was 90% of the reason for the company's dramatic turnaround.

8. Set a goal for the average grade for all meetings, prepare your culture to start grading meetings, set up the system to capture and track each meeting's grade and watch your meetings and culture start sucking less. John's company set a goal to have meetings that were 9s (it seems hardly anyone ever gives a grade of 10).

9. Once you are achieving your goals, go back to the criteria you came up with in item 4 to see if you want to grade meetings based on other important criteria. This helps continuously improve meetings and build good communication muscles.

10. Most important, do what works for you and your company. Take it seriously, don't get defensive about feedback and don't water down this process so much that people roll their eyes at the hypocrisy of this exercise. Take action to make meetings better. Getting everyone in the company involved can create a sense of getting better together, and getting honest about meetings can open up ideas for many more improvements.

Problem Predicting: Build These Muscles to
Avoid This Tough Situation in the Future

The real growth comes from surviving these situations, and then—instead of putting your head down until the next crisis—building processes and systems that prevent the problem from happening again.

To avoid communication breakdown in the future, clarity is key. When you're clear about your company's values, goals and direction, it's easier to make sure your team is truly on board. For example, think about giving a speech or taking a test. Both are stressful, but when you're intimately familiar with the topic or know the answers, this clarity alleviates that stress. If it continues to be difficult, you must figure out what's missing: Do you just not understand, are the goals not clear or do the goals not even exist? Those are three totally different issues that require different responses.

- If you haven't created a strategic plan yet, make this a priority—now. A solid plan that outlines three or five bigger strategic goals, performance metrics to determine if you're heading in the right direction and the short-term actions required in the next one to three months to get there. It should be simple, it should fit on one page and it should be clearly communicated to all employees. This informs every single person in the company where they fit into the overall goals, keeping them focused on what's most important.
- Resist the temptation to create a new communication tool, such as a company newsletter. Another means of communication won't solve the problem; indeed, it sometimes adds a new layer of confusion. A newsletter or

another meeting is a bandage, not a long-term solution. And you don't want to distract the team from focusing on their core contribution to the company goals. Internal newsletters never turned any company into a market leader.

- Every time you schedule a meeting or conversation, ask yourself how it furthers your company's goals. If it doesn't, ask yourself if it's truly necessary.
- Talk to your leadership team and help them understand how to clarify their employees' roles in the overall company strategic plan. Create an open dialogue in which people can admit if they don't understand the direct correlation. You can't have clear communication without honesty and transparency.

So What? Now What?

Poor communication is often cited as a problem, but it's actually a symptom of something else. Communication breaks down when the way forward is unclear, when leaders cannot be trusted, when there is a culture of saying one thing and doing another and/or when chaos and uncertainty reign. Clarify your goals and hold your leaders accountable for communicating the goals on a regular basis so that everyone in your organization can clearly and simply tell you the goals and how they will be achieved.

And don't be afraid to be redundant. When you hear yourself saying the same things over and over, it likely means you're doing it right. A CEO I know never leaves a meeting without reiterating the core goals of the company: to make clients successful and to dominate a specific vertical by optimizing performance, doing the right things in the right ways—always.

THE NINTH WARNING SIGN OF SUCCESS: **INCENTIVIZING FAILURE**

KNOW THIS: Many companies make incentives complicated; instead, keep it simple. It should be easy for every team member to calculate his or her own incentive. The incentive should be tied to the right outcomes (so if the team member wins, the business is winning simultaneously), and team members should be able to figure out how to give themselves a raise by improving the bottom line of the business, directly or indirectly. Incentives do not make mediocre team members great or manipulate people to work harder in ways they wouldn't anyway. The right incentives help great team members focus on the right things. Remember: If everyone on the team focuses on the right things, the entire business succeeds.

FEEL THIS: If you feel like incentives "cost" you every quarter, you're likely incentivizing the wrong things. Getting incentives right is really hard, it takes a lot of patience and some trial and error . . . and it's worth it! If you're doing it right, incentives more than pay for themselves; there is a real return on investment.

DO THIS: There are thousands of ways to incentivize your team; truly the sky is the limit. Make sure your team knows the goal and purpose of incentives, and keep tweaking until you get something that works, for them and for the business. This is where you better have *earned the benefit of the doubt* and trust of your team. If you have to tweak the plan, you will not be successful unless you have earned this critical leadership asset! Take the time to ensure that you're focusing on the *right* incentives and motivating the right behaviors. This could be the biggest profit builder you focus on this year!

If management compensation isn't tied to the right metrics, you may actually be rewarding mediocrity—or even failure. Incentives that don't motivate, drive the right behaviors or produce the desired outcomes erode employee confidence—and keep you off course. Tie compensation directly to what matters most to get everyone headed in the right direction.

I have a friend who worked for a Fortune 500 company, and each quarter—no matter what she did—she got a bonus. It added up to approximately $20,000 a year, so it was substantial. The calculation was based on some arcane, mysterious formula comprised of job level, seniority and the phases of the moon—it was impossible to decipher what she would receive. It was bad for the company because she had the same bonus structure as a mediocre employee. It was bad for her because she never knew what she could do to get a bigger bonus—and she would've done whatever it took! The end result was really just a money pit for the company—the bonus had no impact on her performance.

There's also the opposite effect, which I see all too often in sales organizations: Team members get incentives plus extra praise *plus* extra incentives on top of that. For example, the salesperson who closes a deal gets to keep his job, gets a bonus and gets publicly lauded by the company. Meanwhile, the marketing person who raised awareness to get the prospect's attention and created the tools to help close the deal and the legal team that worked overnight to finalize the agreement all make the same salaries, regardless of their efforts.

It's easier to determine sales incentives than incentives for other types of employees, so most companies pay commissions, but this structure risks alienating the rest of the teams—and all the teams are important, or they wouldn't be part of your business. The average employee will do just the work that's requested of him. But tie incentives to specific activities and measurements, and great team members will know where to focus so they can and will do much more.

Warning Signs: How Do You Know
If You're Incentivizing Failure?

Pay attention—really pay attention—to these warning signs. Do you see yourself in here anywhere?

- Your employees make more and more money each year, but they're not contributing anything extra to the business.
- You cannot answer this question: What is the return on investment of your incentive program?
- You set up an elaborate incentive program to attract an executive from a much larger company, but he's not delivering value to the bottom line. Worse, he got a special deal that breeds resentment in the rest of the team.
- You have incentive payments that go out automatically because it's too difficult to figure out a performance-based amount each quarter.
- You believe that, if the company succeeds, everyone should get a "fair" cut, so you've created a system based solely on tenure.
- Team members see their bonuses as a foregone conclusion—something they expect, rather than earn. This creates an unintended consequence of entitlement.
- Employees couldn't sit at their desks and determine, on their own, precisely how they can get a raise.

Root Cause: Here's the *Real* Problem

So why are you incentivizing failure? Your resources are limited, especially dollars that could otherwise go toward increasing growth or paying off debt. And why do your team members assume they'll get a bonus no matter what?

Let's look at some root causes of this warning sign.

- Your teams don't understand precisely what they must do to help the company meet or exceed its goals. This goes back to having a strategic plan that's easy for team members to understand and that explains precisely how team members' work impacts the goals—every day, every quarter, every year.
- You don't understand yourself what real success means for each function. If your accounting department was able to receive payments 30 days earlier and pay bills 30 days later, what would that do to your cash flow? How does marketing efficiency translate to faster close rates for sales?
- You have goals and metrics in place, but they are not clear. Team members don't know how to impact the metrics they're evaluated on. (Read the eleventh warning sign of success, Random Acts of Accountability, to see why team members don't meet their goals. Here's a hint: They don't know how, they can't, or they won't.) Sometimes goals are so audacious that nobody believes they can ever reach them. If goals feel unattainable, some people never even try.
- Team members don't have control over the goals set for them, so they may attain their part, but if the company as a whole doesn't reach the overall goal, they don't get rewarded. For example, the marketing team exceeds their goal of generating and passing qualified leads to sales, but the sales team doesn't close the deals possible, so they miss their sales projections. If the marketing team exceeded their goals, do they still get rewarded? You can see how these goals are intrinsically connected, but it's critical to have a clear way to reward and incentivize the

right behaviors. Some may be individual and some may be company-wide—be sure to strike the right balance.

Problem Solving: Triage Your Current Situation

Eventually you'll get out of this mode, but right now you have a crisis: You're clearly incentivizing mediocre or even bad work. Maybe you set up incentives in reaction to a previous crisis, so they made sense at the time. But right now, for example, you may be bleeding cash to those who don't deserve it while your best team members are leaving because of poor incentives.

- Get clear on your situation: What's the actual cost of incentives, as a percentage of your overall expenses? How many team members are being overpaid? How many good team members are potentially leaving because they're not properly incentivized?
- What are your core business goals? If you're clear about precisely where you want your business to go, you can more easily get clear on the types of activities that should be rewarded.
- With that in mind, examine what you're rewarding. Was your database a mess, so you incented the sales team to clean it up? What you really want to reward is data accuracy so that cleanup isn't necessary in the future. Did you consider giving incentives for proper training and updated systems that the operations team worked for months to put in place?
- Be open and authentic. Help team members understand that each of them has a direct impact on the success of the business and that you want to help them realize success beyond their wildest dreams. Remember, when individuals

succeed at the right goals, the entire organization succeeds. Nothing breeds success like success!

Problem Predicting: Build These Muscles to Avoid This Tough Situation in the Future

Why do union workers go on strike? It's usually because of money, benefits or both. As an employee, there's nothing worse than having your compensation changed negatively—especially if the change is unpredicable. While your business may not involve unions, you still want to keep your team focused on doing great work—not trying to figure out their bonuses or looking for a higher-paying job.

Incentive plans vary by types of businesses and roles within organizations, but here are some basic guidelines for setting up effective programs.

- With your company's strategic goals in front of you, work with your leadership team to outline precisely how each function directly impacts each goal. Determine what success actually looks like, and what "exceeding expectations" means. Be as specific as possible.
- Determine, as best you can, what great performance brings to the table, or what poor performance detracts from the rest of the business. If you're incenting marketing to get 3,000 leads a quarter, but you're closing only 2% of them, your sales team may be wasting its time on junk. What are the "right" leads worth to the business, and how can you reward marketing for delivering them more efficiently? Think about this for every function in your organization.
- Ask top team members what they think they should be rewarded for. This helps you see if they understand how

their day-to-day work impacts the bottom line, plus it gives you new ideas. Maybe extra days off are more valuable to team members than cash.

- There's a reason sales incentives are so popular—they're straightforward. In general, salespersons have a dollar amount they must sell. But is there anything else that's important that isn't incentivized by that metric? For example, are you incenting them to gain a lot of new clients at smaller revenues, or fewer clients at higher revenues? What if they make deals that perhaps never should have been made, and the client de-books in a few months? Are salespeople still rewarded for that? Get very clear on precisely what you want to reward, and stick with it. Are your best salespeople meeting their goals? If not, why not?

So What? Now What?

When you incent team members for the right things, in the right ways, you'll gain valued team members, give them clear purpose and naturally weed out needless behaviors. When people know that they'll gain more by doing the right things, they'll do the right things—and not get bogged down in unnecessary activities that deplete focus.

The longer you keep good team members, the less time you spend finding and training more team members, and the less time you'll spend on crises overall. A focused incentive program helps keep the entire team—and your business—on track.

NINE

PERFORMANCE

THE FINAL THREE WARNING
SIGNS OF SUCCESS

DON'T FLY BLIND! IT DOESN'T TAKE A CRYSTAL BALL TO DE-termine when your organization is straying from the path to prog-ress. In fact, your organization is full of visible signs of growth or demise, of success or failure, if only you'll take the time and look around.

In this final section, we'll examine this question: What is our performance really telling us about future growth?

THE TENTH WARNING SIGN OF SUCCESS:
THE FALSE SECURITY OF REVENUES

KNOW THIS: Proving you have a valuable product or service and can sell it is critical to the success of any business. Do not let the party of increased revenues leave you with a hangover from the unintended consequences of a rookie entrepreneurial move. You must match increased revenues with the discipline of implementing a financial model that balances the building of profit, equity and cash flow. It can be a rude awakening to realize that as revenues go up, you and your team are unknowingly letting your expenses and cost structure outpace your ability to build a sustainable business model that provides the necessary cash flow to fund future growth.

FEEL THIS: It's natural to want to relax once sales have increased and stabilized. You've worked hard to get here; you deserve it, right? But your relaxation may put your entire business at risk. Stay vigilant. Growing bigger happens only when the bottom line—not the top line—gets bigger.

DO THIS: Make sure you have strong financial forecasting tools, and pressure-test the accuracy of your forecasts. It is okay to dominate a market by delaying profitability, but *not* at the expense of building a financial model that can support the weight of future growth. Take an honest look at your situation. Have tough conversations. Be brave enough to be brutally honest about the situation, and move forward with purpose.

Things look good; you're focused on revenues, naturally, and they're growing. But you let this lull you into a false sense of security—and now expenses are starting to grow faster than revenues. You don't have all the financial, performance or market data you need to predict problems—or you don't know how to analyze the data you have.

It's time to combine sophisticated processes with rigorous analysis of the right metrics.

While this may seem like an accounting issue, it goes far, far beyond this—and if you're in this situation, you know how scary and draining it can be. You thought you were flying high, but it turns out you were flying right into the side of a mountain.

And this is so much more common than most people think. Time and again, I've seen smart entrepreneurs confront what I call "threading the eye of the needle."

Threading the Needle

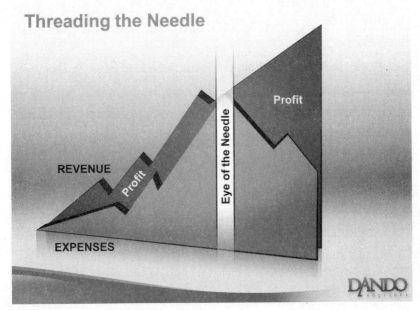

Figure 17

Again, their success—great revenues—is the very harbinger of their downfall when they can't bridge this gap. It is not intuitive, but while you are building revenues and repeatable sales processes, you are simultaneously *not* building the critical muscles to monitor and forecast expenses and return on investment.

It is like a body builder who develops only his upper body but has skinny little legs. Many entrepreneurs do not like the hard work of building a good base. Your huge muscles in one area could topple you completely if you're not careful.

When cash flow gets tight, the fun part of growing the business goes out the window, and finger-pointing and infighting take over. It feels impossible to move forward; in spite of all the great sales growth, failure seems imminent.

Private equity firms and other would-be buyers look for companies in the eye of the needle. While this is not the term they use, the dynamic is something they all recognize. They know exactly which emotional buttons to push so that you're ready to sell when they're ready to buy—your company at pennies on the dollar.

What does everyone in the company fear after it has been sold? That the new owners are going to come in and "clean house," and a lot of people are going to suffer. And why do the new owners do this? It's not because they're mean or have their own special people they like, or any other sweet little lies we may tell ourselves. They're simply putting into place the right leadership, management and systems to take the organization from a Level 2 company to a Level 3 company. Unfortunately, the very people who helped grow the company get lost in the shuffle—because buyers take emotion out of the equation in order to put the company back on course.

Fact is, *you can do this work yourself* and keep much of your team and culture intact. Financial reporting and modeling are not rocket science; they're just math. I understand that math can be intimidating, but the beauty is that it's absolute. There's no justification or emotion or gray area. Having a good financial person on the team should give you the skills and experience you need to steer your company in the right direction.

We've all known about or even worked for companies that didn't make it through the eye of the needle—they had massive layoffs, were bought cheap by competitors or just went under. It's absolutely critical to solve this problem, and it's impossible to become a Level 3 business until you bridge this gap or, even better, avoid it altogether. Working through this stressful process dramatically slows your growth, so the earlier you catch it, the better.

For example, remember that company I mentioned earlier in chapter 4, with a $250,000 tax bill coming due, and they didn't have the money? This was a company that was profitable and doing well, but this unexpected cost, they thought, could crush them. When I looked into the situation, I pointed out the extra inventory in the warehouse that could easily cover the debt. A "fire sale" paid their taxes and bought them time. They put a financial professional in place to create the systems and foresight they needed to keep growing with a balanced approach to increasing profits, equity and cash flow.

Any company can get into this situation, even if they're not feeling the pinch of expenses outweighing revenues—yet. I worked with a company that did $100 million in annual sales and had always been profitable, growing steadily year over year. They had been very financially responsible, but the owner was at a point where he couldn't get a bigger line of credit. He was also getting older, so it was getting harder for him to justify guaranteeing everything himself. A solid financial professional could have helped wean the company off this situation much earlier, taking much of the pressure off the owner.

Fact is, *finances are wildly predictable.* Math doesn't lie. It doesn't assign names of friends to each line item. It represents only the facts, and as an entrepreneur, you need those facts to counterbalance your passion for your business and your team. The right financial professional will offer options for thorny issues and help you see down the road so you avoid future financial surprises.

Think about it this way: Running your business without solid financial data systems, forecasting and planning is like driving 80 miles an hour down a freeway in reverse using only the rearview mirror to guide you. Sure, it *could* work, but moving forward with a full, clear windshield is much safer—not to mention more comfortable.

Warning Signs: How Do You Know If
You Have a False Security of Revenues?

Pay attention—really pay attention—to these warning signs. Do you see yourself in here anywhere?

- Your expenses are increasing at a rate greater than your revenues, yet this imbalance is either unnoticed or elaborately justified.
- The seduction of increased revenues blinds you and your team to the decay of an unsustainable financial model.
- You're not sure how much money you need to fund your current and future growth. You do not have a reliable system for cash flow forecasting.
- You consistently miss forecasts and/or are short of cash.
- You keep approving extra spending in the *hope* that you will generate enough revenues in the future to cover it.
- You don't have a solid grasp of your actual costs of doing business and how these scale—or don't—with your business.
- You don't have a clear, detailed correlation between revenues and costs.
- You're currently considering cutting team members, downsizing offices, or making other major cuts because of *unexpected or unplanned* losses or shortages of cash.

Root Cause: Here's the *Real* Problem

So why is this happening? When you get to the root cause—the "why"—you can take effective action. Be patient, because this can take some focused thinking and honest conversations. But you can't move forward until you truly understand the root cause.

- You do not have the right financial person on your team. Justify it all you want, but this is a completely predictable problem that the right financial guidance would never allow or enable!

- You don't have the right data, processes or systems in place to truly understand your costs in relation to revenues. Until you dig in deep—including variable costs, fixed costs, and what it truly takes to financially run the business—you'll never be able to confidently state that your costs and revenues are in line.

- You've been growing so quickly that you've allowed accounting to get out of control, ignoring critical details. You've allowed revenues to be your sole signal for success.

- Your leadership team—including yourself—doesn't have a firm grasp on the true cause-and-effect relationship between the balance sheet and profit-and-loss statements.

- You've purposely ignored financial warning signs, hoping that high revenue growth would solve all your financial woes at some unspecified future point.

Problem Solving: Triage Your Current Situation

Soon you'll get out of problem-solving mode because you'll build your problem-predicting muscles—and you won't find yourself in this situation again. For now, though, you need quick solutions to get you out of this immediate situation. Remember: We get what we set ourselves up for. Take a moment to honestly assess where you are right now, so you can move ahead with purpose.

- Determine the real root cause or causes from the list above—the causes, not just the symptoms. Getting clarity here helps you solve the problem.

- Once you understand the real problem, find creative ways to deal with it. For example, if you have a short-term cash flow problem, is there extra inventory you could sell, or could you work with vendors to push payments back? Again, these are short-term solutions, but they may keep you on your feet until you address the larger problem.
- If your team doesn't understand the cause-and-effect relationship between a balance sheet and a profit-and-loss statement, it's time to get educated—while it's still cheap, before you get a very expensive education!

Problem Predicting: Build These Muscles to Avoid This Tough Situation in the Future

The real growth comes from surviving these situations, and then—instead of putting your head down until the next crisis—building processes and systems that prevent the problem from happening again. *If you take your team out of problem-solving mode, they'll use their brain cells to innovate and move the business forward—where you want it to go.*

- You must have a proven and capable financial person on your team who can develop and effectively communicate the key performance metrics that can help you and your team forecast accurately and act accordingly.
- The company must consistently meet a set of financial goals balanced among profit, cash flow and equity building.
- You must establish debt-to-equity objectives and monitor performance regularly.
- Ensure that systems are in place that clearly illustrate (measure) how limited resources (money and time) are spent.

- Verify that expenditures are in line with the priorities and goals of the company.
- Make budgeting an integral part of the company culture.
- Be sure that key performance metrics are established, monitored and timely.

So What? Now What?

Get your financial house in order. If you don't know where to start, find an experienced, trusted accountant or business consultant to look at your business objectively—not emotionally—to help you understand all the ins and outs of your balance sheet, profit-and-loss statement and all other necessary financial forecasting tools.

I get it; as an entrepreneur, finances may not be your "thing." But I also know that you're responsible for customers, team members, your office rent and more—not to mention your own family's well-being.

You want to avoid the eye of the needle if at all possible. If you don't, at best you'll delay your growth and come out of the gap battered and bruised. At worst, you'll lose it all.

It's just that simple.

THE ELEVENTH WARNING SIGN OF SUCCESS:
RANDOM ACTS OF ACCOUNTABILITY

KNOW THIS: Great leaders create cultures of motivating accountability so everyone knows what winning looks like. Winners *want* measurable goals so they can see exactly where they are at any time. The key to motivation is a sense of accomplishment, and this requires measuring progress. There are four specific reasons people do not do what they're supposed to do; they are covered in this section. The first step to creating accountability is to be personally accountable.

FEEL THIS: You can walk into any organization and quickly sense if there is a high level of motivating accountability or a culture of creating excuses. Excuses are like drugs: They deteriorate performance, it's very hard to stop the habit and people do not stop using them until there is a train wreck. Many people think the only way to hold someone accountable is with punitive actions (e.g., firing someone); this is not true! Creating accountability can feel awkward, can feel like conflict, can even feel scary, but the consequence of not being personally accountable or creating a culture of accountability is a fool's journey to chaos!

DO THIS: Hire people who are personally accountable. Pressure-test this characteristic in the hiring process and build it into review cycles. Do not negotiate or make excuses for yourself or anyone else. To win, you owe it to your team, customers and investors to be clear about what winning looks like and to create a culture where people are personally accountable. Look at your strategic plan and determine exactly what success means for each of the functions in your organization. Clarity at this level helps you make good decisions across your team.

Your business isn't moving forward because it's not clear to every team member exactly how their jobs align with specific company goals. There's no transparent, consistent culture of positive accountability, so great team members flounder and less-than-great team members use the blurred expectations to their advantage. It's critical that you, as the leader, understand and communicate corporate goals and illustrate how everyone's specific efforts create larger success.

People often think that the only way to hold others account-able is to threaten or fire them. But the real truth is that the best way to motivate people is to make them responsible for them-selves. When performance metrics are in place, it helps all your team members prioritize what's truly important. Great team members will get really focused and exceed expectations. Medio-cre team members may rise to the occasion, change roles to make a more tangible impact or self-select out of the business. And poor performers will be aware, every day, that they're falling short. If they don't improve, the data makes their transition from the busi-ness a fairly simple exercise. They'll likely quit before you have to fire them, paving the way for true rock stars to take their place. And presto, you have a culture of motivating accountability.

Companies also tend to reward people for *solving problems,* but not *predicting* and therefore *avoiding them* in the first place. Give special thought to this—are you rewarding your sales team for simply making up for last quarter's shortfall, or must they make up for last quarter *and* this quarter in order to reap any rewards? Is that sustainable, possible or fair? Is there a problem with the forecasting model that caused the shortfall? Consider all the angles so you're not just solving a short-term problem.

I worked with a company that spent millions of dollars on marketing due to a strong-willed, uncontrollable executive. For years, the rest of the executive team challenged this person to illustrate the return on this marketing investment. When the ex-ecutive finally exited the business, new metrics-focused leadership emerged, and though it took months to integrate the sales and marketing systems along with a complicated database, within a year the team was finally able to see their exact impact on closed deals. The information gleaned gave the marketing team the pre-cise information they needed to buy the right media, target the right audiences and make the right decision about every dollar they spent.

Today the marketing and sales teams work closely to continuously improve the leads that emerge from the marketing machine, and team members can see precisely how their activities impact the business. This level of accountability—one that many marketing teams aspire to but few attain—has actually motivated the rock stars on the marketing team, rather than making them feel the "pressure" to meet quotas.

Warning Signs: How Do You Know If Your Accountability Measures Are Random?

Pay attention—really pay attention—to these warning signs. Do you see yourself in here anywhere?

- You consistently hear rumblings about how poor accountability is in the organization. Or everyone lights up when you talk about getting training for conflict resolution, how to have difficult conversations or how to improve accountability—because they think it is something everyone else needs, not them.
- There are excuses layered upon excuses about why important work is not getting done, to the point that it feels impossible to tell fact from fiction.
- Your team members are technically meeting their goals— their stated objectives are reached—but the business isn't moving forward.
- You or your team members, when asked, don't understand how their roles tie directly into the strategic goals of the company.

- Your top performers report frustration with co-workers who don't pull their weight.
- There is frequent turnover in a key role or team.

Root Cause: Here's the *Real* Problem

So why is this happening? There are four reasons people don't meet their goals:

1. *Goals. The first issue is about the actual* goals—*or the lack thereof.* One of these situations usually exists:
   - There are no clear goals. You really must create your strategic plan. Really.
   - Goals are not realistic. They are not based in reason or data.
   - The team doesn't really buy into the goals. This is usually symptomatic of a culture where those who speak up against new ideas are considered "bad eggs." You must create an environment of authenticity and transparency, where people can share their opinions respectfully. And the absolutely only place this can start is at the very top—with you and the executives that surround you. There is no way around this; you must get honest with yourself and everyone else.
   - The goals and metrics change so frequently that team members lose faith that the leadership actually knows what they are doing.
2. *Communication. Team members* don't know *what they are supposed to do.* They either don't know how their work specifically fits into the company's goals, or they don't know how to reach those goals. Goals or objectives

may change so frequently that no one can tell what winning looks like or means anymore. It's up to leadership to clarify this, set up specific metrics, and coach team members to success. Notice that I said "coach," because this is not a one-and-done proposition. A coach is there during the key moments of the game, during practice and even during off hours. A team member who doesn't "get it" needs your leadership to help them understand what the expectations are and needs to be able to clearly communicate them back to you. Then you need to follow up and check up with them until they have proven they have mastered the skill and outcome you desire. Remember, people do not do what you expect, they do what you inspect. Once they have proven to have the skill then you can trust them to get the desired outcomes without so much checking in. If the goals don't seem to be sinking in, ask team members how you might better communicate the goals.

3. *Abilities or resources. Team members* can't *do what is being asked of them.* Team members don't have the skills, talent or tools to reach the goals. It's actually mean to put employees in this position; you must make sure that the goals are attainable and within the team members' power and that the team is set up for success. I've often seen leaders put a team member in a no-win situation, then keep the person there out of guilt. They look the other way until it gets so bad that the leader reacts out of anger or disgust. That's not leadership; that's cowardice.

4. *Laziness. Team members* won't *do what is being asked of them.* This is where a lot of employers *assume* their team members are lazy or incompetent. Do your best to avoid

getting to this late stage. This can happen when a good team member is worn-out or burned-out because he or she has spent years chasing unattainable or shifting goals. But it can also happen when team members feel the work is beneath them or other conditions have created hostility.

If it's truly a case of insubordination or laziness, you want to move that person out of his or her position as quickly as possible; holding on to this employee risks poisoning the rest of the team. Your rock stars will quickly notice this person slacking and blame management for not taking action. Letting a nonperformer stay in a position degrades everyone's work and will quickly drive your top performers into the arms of another, more accountability-focused organization.

This is where the "Do I have the right person?" conversation effectively always ends. Remember these two points when people consistently do not do what you asked or what you expected:

1. They either
   a. don't know how, or
   b. can't, or
   c. won't.
2. Based on the answer to question 1, then you have to decide to
   a. train them,
   b. transfer them to positions where they can succeed, or
   c. terminate them.

Most of these are *leadership issues,* not necessarily performance issues. It's up to the leadership—and specifically the person's direct managerial leader—to determine which of these is true for each team member who is not performing up to expectations. For obvious reasons, the easiest case to address is when team members don't know what they are supposed to do. When you bring clarity about how the work fits into the bigger picture and put clear metrics in place, it's much easier to identify deeper problems.

Problem Solving: Triage Your Current Situation

Soon you'll get out of problem-solving mode because you'll build your problem-predicting muscles—and you won't find yourself in this situation again. For now, though, you need quick solutions to get you out of this immediate situation.

- Determine where you're weak in metrics, and start there. If you lack accountability across the whole business, start in the areas that will have the most immediate, visible impact, such as sales, accounts receivable and customer acquisition.
- If you are measuring the right metrics, dig in to understand why a team or team member isn't performing, based on the four criteria described in the previous section. Take quick action accordingly.
- Don't operate in a vacuum. Turn to your leaders' experience to determine what's most important and how to measure it. Sales will naturally have different goals than customer service, but they may be able to use similar tools to measure success.
- Make sure you're measuring the right things—in the short term and the long term. For example, it may

be critical for the sales team to increase sales 40% in the fourth quarter, but long-term strategy is just as important. What does the team need to do in the coming year, and what metrics should be put in place now to keep everyone on track? Make sure you are building the right muscles.

Problem Predicting: Build These Muscles to Avoid This Tough Situation in the Future

The real growth comes from surviving these situations, and then—instead of putting your head down until the next crisis—building processes and systems that prevent the problem from happening again.

To avoid making accountability seem punitive—"Do this or you're fired!"—help team members understand how their daily work fits into the company's goals. And clearly communicate the timing you expect for progress to start to appear in the metrics, so momentum doesn't slow. As a leadership team, you may ultimately determine that you need more time, but it's important to set a goal—for both metrics and time—to keep you honest.

- Look at the business's overall goals as a whole, then tap into exactly how each role fits into the goals. It should become crystal clear exactly what the metrics for success are.
- Every day provides an opportunity to win, lose or draw. If everyone on your team cannot clearly understand what a win is, they are just playing hard rather than playing to win. This is overly obvious and embarrassingly simple, but not easy. If your sales leadership is working to close

100 deals—at any price point—this quarter, but you've promised Wall Street a specific revenue number, you may be wearing out the sales team for nothing. Get clear. Over-communicate if needed. Be specific. Make sure nothing is lost in translation.

- Involve the team in the process of defining performance metrics. Sometimes employees can't reach their goals because they're dependent on a function those employees can't control. Keep asking questions to ensure the metrics are attainable and fair. The goals may be a stretch, and that's fine—winners actually expect this. But teams should have the basic resources to meet their goals.

- You may determine that you need different skill sets on your team to reach your goals. If so, create a list of specific business skills and experience necessary to effectively meet your desired metrics. For example, if the business goal is to lead a sales team that grows sales 120% over the next five years, find someone who has achieved this in a similarly sized company. When looking at prospective hires, focus on these skills (and confirm that they have a history of being personally accountable); they're either there or they're not. If they're not, don't equivocate: They're not a fit. Move on. Remember, we get what we set ourselves up for. Think about your sales team right now. Has each leader previously attained a similar goal elsewhere? Or have you just promoted your best, longest-tenured salespeople to management? Sales are so critical to a business; you cannot afford to *hope* they rise to the occasion.

- Strive to look beyond short-term goals. All too often, I see companies setting goals in the same quarter they want them to be attained! This creates only a to-do list, not a growth strategy. Think out at least a year—though five years is even better.

So What? Now What?

It all comes back to your strategic plan. You must have a set of goals that are clear and that each team can contribute to, even if they don't have a direct impact. For example, your goal may be to sell to every dealership in town, so the accounting team may wonder how they fit in. If they work to make invoicing and payables more efficient or give clients billing options that fit the dealership's business model, they're helping promote this goal.

Accountability makes everyone's expectations crystal clear. When people know what's most important, it helps them focus on those things first, helping to ensure they're working on the right projects—not just the ones that are easiest. When team members see how their direct contribution helps reach the bigger corporate goals, accountability becomes a positive—not a negative.

THE TWELFTH WARNING SIGN OF SUCCESS:
SOWING THE SEEDS OF DECAY

KNOW THIS: The systems and processes you created in the beginning that have allowed you to grow and be successful may not only *not* fit your organization anymore; they may be killing it. They may be legacy processes or systems that are the exact reason you were able to grow. It is not intuitively obvious that the very things that made you successful are now sowing the seeds of your decay.

FEEL THIS: It's extremely emotional to change processes and systems mid-flight. When you find out that the engines on your plane (in this case the systems and processes) will not get you to where you want to go and you cannot land the plane (stop what you are doing) to fix them, it can be extremely intimidating—so much so that you and your leadership team do not even allow yourselves to consider the overly obvious and embarrassingly simple (but not easy) repairs you need to keep your company on track and out of the weeds. Nobody wants to switch out an engine on a plane at 30,000 feet—it's easier to just *hope* you do not fly into a mountain. You and your team can waste a lot of time trying to create incremental improvements that sow the seeds of decay.

DO THIS: Be brave. Understand that change is hard, people won't like it and it will take time, with good predicting and lots of communicating. It is a process, and it can be painful. But it's critical to continued growth. Be willing to exchange "Do it fast—keep hitting the numbers!" for "Do it right!"

Your growing company has outgrown your systems and processes—everything from accounting to people to technology. And you may not even know it, because you're so busy focusing on growing revenues or juggling rapid growth. Right under your nose, systems that once enhanced your business may actually be speeding its demise. Learn the signs of system decay—before they derail your progress.

Entrepreneurs are a special breed. To get your new company off the ground, you'll do anything and everything. It's messy, it's fast, it's exciting. There are many, many leaders who thrive in this environment—every day is a high in a high-growth start-up. You see great results—sales are up, new products are created. You don't care how it happened; you're focused on the results. Months down the road, when things slow down, you'll wonder *why* they slowed down. But you won't be able to retrace your steps, because you didn't have any processes in place. The best you can do is guess at what worked and what didn't.

Often, as a start-up gets more established, the leadership team puts the entrepreneurs into offices and has them focus on new ventures, as the company starts to build out processes focused on the main goals of the business—something most entrepreneurs don't want to do. When the "grown-ups" go to check in on the entrepreneurs, the results can be ugly: The entrepreneurs have created their own fiefdoms; they do things differently than any other area of the business; they are bleeding money; and it's unclear when or how they'll get the results they set out for.

A lot of executives I work with say that they're building a plane while it's 30,000 feet in the air. It's not an accident that that sounds so terrifying. Most people feel it's much easier to *hope* they do not fly into a mountain, because actually creating and changing processes that will get you to your destination is *hard work*. Most people don't want to do this and can't see that they're rocketing toward a mountain.

Successful leaders, though, understand the importance and difficulty of replacing the engine (systems and processes). They know that it's the only way they'll survive. And they hire people who will do this hard, dangerous work. They hire people who understand the difference between solving short-term problems and predicting problems and preventing them from happening again.

I recently worked with a company that had been wildly successful but was now faltering badly. The CEO was emotional and way too close to the situation. I quickly saw that each of the company's branch offices was run by an entrepreneurial-type leader, each of whom ran his branch his own way. This had kept the branches agile in the beginning and was the very reason for their early success, but now it was actually speeding the company's demise. It was sowing the seeds of their decay.

Since each branch ran independently, some of them had great processes that were really working, but nothing was shared. They couldn't get consistent data to understand what was truly going on across the business. The company was unable to build on its success and was ultimately reduced to chaos.

We introduced standardized processes into all the businesses, which caused great consternation and even anger. We had to convince the managers that, while it might be painful for them now, it was better, overall, for the whole organization. We were able to turn things around—the company is back to growing top line and bottom line in a predictable and meaningful way—but it was tough. Things had to get worse before they got better, and it took discipline, maturity and a team of leaders who could predict and communicate this to their teams so they could help.

The point of this story is that it's important to put *everything* on the table when faced with a crisis or chaos in the business—even things that have helped you gain success in the first place.

It's a fact: The kind of people who are attracted to start-up life in the first place tend to be impatient, impetuous and excited by chaos. Very few of these people will get excited by the prospect of creating systems and processes that will force them to slow down, be contemplative or worry about a larger system or infrastructure. "Serial entrepreneurs" are called so for a reason—they thrive on starting something, but not so much on sustaining it.

Sometimes the best companies are those where the start-up entrepreneur creates a great business, then steps aside for a more process-oriented CEO to scale it.

Warning Signs: How Do You Know If
You're Sowing the Seeds of Decay?

Pay attention—really pay attention—to these warning signs. Do you see yourself in here anywhere?

- Even though you've been in business for months or years, you and your team are skeptical that the current way of doing business (your systems and processes or platform) will scale to meet the needs of growth.
- The systems and processes that made you successful have never been scrutinized to make sure they are still adding value.
- Your managerial leaders spend more time working *in* the business than *on* the business, so it's unclear whether the current systems and processes can handle the weight of growth.
- The data you need to track your goals either don't exist or are consistently wrong. In short, you don't really know you have the wrong flight plan until you are over the Bermuda Triangle and running out of gas.
- You see that everyone is working really hard, but they still can't tell you what will happen next quarter or next year.
- Problem solving is rewarded, while problem predicting is simply a nice, vague idea.
- You have one-off fiefdoms with leaders that do their own thing outside the structure of the rest of the business. These people aren't necessarily wrong or evil, but you need to understand why they think they need to operate separately. Do they know something you don't know? If they're running their organizations separately, you must

determine if they're right, you're right or there's a middle ground that's best.

Root Cause: Here's the *Real* Problem

So why is this happening? You can't move forward until you truly understand the root cause. Here are some root causes to consider:

- You have systems, processes and ways of doing things that are the exact reasons you and your organization have been successful . . . but maybe they have become legacy systems. You may even be convinced that these ways of operating (such as putting entrepreneurial, sales-minded leaders in place to run your branch offices) or leading (such as an emotionally charged and force-of-will approach) are your secret sauce and are the things you need to hold on to most tightly. It is not intuitively obvious that the very things that made you successful are now causing your demise. It's time to dig into the details, have honest conversations with the leadership team and get to the source of this problem.

- You have entrepreneurs in leadership roles who were great for your start-up, but they don't function well in a process-based, mature organization. Either they must pivot, or you must. A strong entrepreneurial sales leader who was great at inspiring people during the start-up phase may have no idea how to design, implement and monitor the necessary systems and processes needed to grow predictably and forecast accurately.

- You like and respect those who helped you start the company, so you gave them leadership roles that they may no longer fit. Your team was great at starting up, but collectively, you have no experience beyond that.

- Just like your leadership team, you must look at yourself. As CEO, you don't have to be a process person yourself; you just need to understand that process is needed, and then you need to hire someone smarter and more experienced than you to create it.

Problem Solving: Triage Your Current Situation

Soon you'll get out of problem-solving mode because you'll build your problem-predicting muscles—and you won't find yourself in this situation again. For now, though, you need quick solutions to get you out of this immediate situation.

- Get very, very clear on your company goals. They must be measurable. Once you set a number goal, dig in deep to understand the very next steps to attaining that number. It might take brainpower that you, alone, don't have, so get your leadership team involved. Every number must be backed up by a process to reach it. Don't stop until you have dissected every single metric.
- Create processes integral to your success. Break down sales goals by number of leads needed and number of reps necessary, defining the target markets and understanding where they are regionally—all these data points help you create a process for reaching your sales goal.
- Become uniquely focused on implementing processes— creating excellent forecasting tools and dashboards, for example—that help you predict problems instead of waiting for problems to surprise you and force you into action.

- Objectively review any processes you currently have in place with your leadership team. For each existing process, ask these serious questions and document the answers:
  - Does it scale?
  - Will it help us get to our goals?
  - Does it hinge on one person, or can it scale beyond one person?
  - What are the processes that, if we solve them right now, will help us reach our core goals?

This gives you the road map you need to start improving your processes immediately. It will help the entire process feel less daunting, because you'll know exactly where to start and where the finish line is.

Problem Predicting: Build These Muscles to Avoid This Tough Situation in the Future

The real growth comes from surviving these situations, and then—instead of putting your head down until the next crisis—building processes and systems that prevent the problem from happening again.

The muscles you build by carefully reviewing existing processes will help you as you create new ones. Resist the temptation to simply put a bandage on existing processes. Learn to create *only* processes that scale as you imagine your business in the future. Look to large companies to see where they have succeeded—or failed—in their processes.

Understand—and I mean really understand—that you *must* create an engine that will work for your entire journey as a company. You don't want to have to replace the engine in your space shuttle as you head toward the moon. You don't want to have to go through this pain again.

So What? Now What?

I get it—most entrepreneurs cringe at the word "process." It sounds boring and tedious—and it can be. But wouldn't you rather be bored in the short term and wildly successful in the long term? Do you want to burst into flames as you fly into the side of the mountain? Creating processes that scale and take you to the next level is tough work, but it will be some of the most gratifying work you'll do—mainly because you never thought you could do something so difficult. And along the way, you'll find smart people who thrive—even get excited!—about creating scalable processes. Get and hold on to these people; you'll need them.

CONCLUSION

THINK BIG, START SMALL, MOVE FAST!

SO THESE ARE THE FACTS: CRISIS WILL HAPPEN AS GROWTH occurs, particularly when you make the leap from one level of business to another. The way to avoid letting those inflection points become full-blown train wrecks is to anticipate the problems your business will encounter—today and in the future.

Be transparent; don't keep this information to yourself. Let everyone in the company know where you are, where you're headed and what speed bumps you're likely to encounter on your journey.

Transparency about growth, success, pain and warning signs will help your company avoid what I call the Chicken Little Complex. This is exactly what it sounds like—the minute you hit the smallest snag, everyone runs around complaining that the sky is falling.

You must normalize the journey of growth for your team, so they can be part of the solution when these very predictable, very normal consequences of success occur.

HOW TO DEVELOP YOUR PROBLEM-PREDICTING MUSCLES

As I stated earlier, although *how* your business or department grows is as unique as the people in your business, and unique to your market and industry, the *challenges* that growth causes are common to all. In other words, the details may be different but the dynamics of growth are the same. When you see beyond the details, you will see the patterns.

There have been thousands of leaders, businesses and departments in these situations long before now . . . and you can learn from them and normalize your journey. You should be focused on innovating and creating new products and/or services for your customers instead of wasting your team's brainpower identifying and solving problems and challenges that have already been solved by thousands of leaders and their companies long before you!

Make yourself aware of the most common challenges that cause 90% of businesses to level out in their growth, go back and get smaller or worse.

Use these guidelines to help you evolve into a Predictive Leader:

1. *Focus on the vital few and forget the trivial many.* Look for a pattern of recurring challenges. See beyond the details and to the patterns—or, even better, the warning signs of success. You can't eliminate every one right away, so evaluate which are costing customers or employees the most time or money, and start there.

2. *Assess risks through the lens of priorities and opportunities.* Don't obsess over the challenges inherent to a growing business. Instead, get and keep your team focused. Remember, strategy is not only about the 5% you will do. It is also about the 95% you won't.
   - Know what stage of development you are at in the Business Growth Cycle. Ask your team to review this section of the book (chapters 3, 4 and 5), and go through it with them.

- Do a 12-point inspection with each of the 12 Warning Signs of Success with your leadership team. You may gloss over some signs, thinking your team suffers from a select few, but when you get the leadership team involved, they may see things you missed—and this is hugely valuable.

3. *Be specific.* A challenge that's vaguely defined—like "communication problems" or "interruptions"—can't be solved. You must know the who, what, when, where, how and why of these issues. What is the root cause? Challenge team members—and yourself—to get specific about how prevalent problems truly are. But do not fall into the trap of debating the details at the expense of not recognizing the patterns that are hurting you.

4. *Address the root cause of the issue.* Look for the root cause of the issue, not just the symptoms. For example, you may identify a specific communications problem and react by saying "send out a memo." But this rarely gets to the root cause; it's just a quick fix. *Start with "you" before you move to "who."* You don't want to turn your search for the root cause into a finger-pointing or blame game. The first step in getting to the root cause is to ask what you could have done better or differently. Even if it turns out the root cause is another individual, it still comes back to you. It's your job to either help them develop or help them find something else to do.

5. *Involve all those affected.* Rather than run around getting ten different explanations from ten people, get everyone in the same room at the same time. This may not be natural or comfortable, but it's the only way to get anywhere near the truth, especially in highly emotional situations where there is a lot of back-channel manipulation going on. Do

not avoid the conflict entirely, or you will get what you are setting yourself up for.

6. *No back channel.* Never talk negatively about anyone who isn't around. The only exception is if you need to seek outside counsel before confronting the individual, and even then, try to bring that person into the conversation as soon as possible. When you talk negatively about one person to another person, the second person will immediately wonder if you are talking negatively about him or her as well. This is no way to build trust.

SO WHAT? NOW WHAT?

At the beginning of this book I promised you that this book would accomplish five simple, but uniquely vital, goals:

1. You will clearly see and understand the *obvious* and *simple* answers that will help you grow, mature and stabilize your business. You will wonder why you never saw them before!

2. You and your team will become *problem predictors* rather than *problem solvers.* In this chaotic business environment, you have to be able to see around corners and predict problems *before* they show up in the results.

3. You and your team will use your brains for innovating new products and services to serve your market, instead of wasting your time and IQ points solving problems that have already been solved in thousands of other businesses.

4. You will *redefine* what leadership and the journey to business growth look like for you, your team and your business, creating a wealth that is far more satisfying than money alone.

5. You and your team will *unlock* the opportunities you have been missing, so together you can build a business that *grows* and *changes the world*.

I hope I delivered on that promise. (And if not, I've love to hear where I failed and how.)

I would also love to hear about the warning signs of success you discovered in your own organization, what you did about them and how you made this book actionable. To aid in those efforts, I've designed a website specifically for this book at www .kirkdando.com. Here you'll find additional resources to help you put the book into action, matrices to fill out, bonus content and frequent updates. You'll also find downloadable tools you can use no matter the size of the company, level of business or warning sign of success you're struggling with.

If you want to dig deeper into each warning sign of success, read up-to-the-minute blog posts about how other companies deal with these warning signs, or simply ask a question or drop by www.kirkdando.com and join the discussion.

And don't hide this light under a bushel! If you've found this book helpful, share it with your entire team—your leadership and future leaders—and your colleagues who may be suffering themselves.

Remember, you're not in this alone. Thousands of leaders have been here before you. Learn from their mistakes instead of suffering through your own. It's the best way to become the market leader your company is meant to be!

NOTES

PART I

1. John Maxwell, "Meet John," The John Maxwell Co. (2013), http://www .johnmaxwell.com/about/meet-john/.

PART II

1. Larry E. Greiner, "Evolution and Revolution as Organizations Grow," *Harvard Business Review* (1972 and 1998), http://hbr.org/1998/05 /evolution-and-revolution-as-organizations-grow/ar/1.
2. Robert Beale, "About Beale International," Beale International Inc., (2009), http://www.bealeinternational.com/.

CHAPTER 6

1. HBR IdeaCast, "Good Strategy's Non-Negotiables," HBR Blog Network (March 15, 2012), http://blogs.hbr.org/2012/03/good-strategys -non-negotiables/.
2. Ibid.
3. Ibid.
4. Ibid.

CHAPTER 7

1. Zig Ziglar, *Raising Positive Kids in a Negative World,* Nashville: Thomas Nelson (2002).
2. Fast Company Staff, "Dick Costolo and Ben Horowitz on the Give and Take of Taking the Reins," *Fast Company* (January 15, 2013), http:// www.fastcompany.com/3004363/dick-costolo-and-ben-horowitz-give -and-take-taking-reins.
3. Ibid.
4. Ibid.

INDEX